Au aug 13

LONG BEACH WILD

adrienne **MASON**

LONG BEACH
WILD

*A Celebration of People and Place on
Canada's Rugged Western Shore*

GREYSTONE BOOKS

D&M PUBLISHERS INC.
Vancouver/Toronto/Berkeley

Greystone Books
An imprint of D&M Publishers Inc.
2323 Quebec Street, Suite 201
Vancouver BC Canada V5T 4S7
www.greystonebooks.com

Cataloguing data available from Library and Archives Canada
ISBN 978-1-55365-344-8 (pbk.)
ISBN 978-1-926812-68-7 (ebook)

Editing by Georgina Montgomery and Lara Kordic
Cover and text design by Heather Pringle
Maps by Marion Syme
Cover photograph by Stephen Strathdee/Getty Images
Photographs are the property of individual photographers
and rights holders found on page 205
Printed and bound in Canada by Friesens
Text printed on acid-free, 30% post-consumer paper
Distributed in the U.S. by Publishers Group West

We gratefully acknowledge the financial support of the Canada Council
for the Arts, the British Columbia Arts Council, the Province of British
Columbia through the Book Publishing Tax Credit, and the Government
of Canada through the Canada Book Fund for our publishing activities.

Contents

To my family, Patrice, Ava and Bob, as always.
And in memory of Marilyn and Neil Buckle.
Fabulous storytellers, gone far too soon.

"I loved every bit of it—no boundaries, no beginning, no end, one continual shove of growing—edge of land meeting edge of water, with just a ribbon of sand between. Sometimes the ribbon was smooth, sometimes fussed with foam. Trouble was only on the edges; both sea and forests in their depths were calm and still. Virgin soil, clean sea, pure air, vastness by day, still deeper vastness in dark when beginnings and endings join." EMILY CARR, *Growing Pains: An Autobiography*

"But be warned ... this outer edge of Canada is lonely, exciting, and unforgettable. It is a disease. It may fill your comfortable life with restlessness." R.M.O. MCMINN, *Island Events*, June 20, 1952

introduction
flood tide

WINTER SOLSTICE at Long Beach: what better place to mark the first official day of the dark season? A walk here is an early gift I've granted myself, time snatched away from my desk and to-do list for the upcoming holiday. I begin at a spot we call "Incinerator." The tide is flooding, and because the December 21 solstice brings some of the year's highest tides, only a sliver of beach is left between the rising water and the barricade of logs at the forest's edge. It will be a quick jaunt.

I see no other cars in the parking lot. And even if there were some, the sixteen kilometres (ten miles) of open, clean sand beach sweeping off to my right and left is more than enough to share. Still, I feel unrepentantly smug. All of this is just for me.

1

In the summer, this section of the beach swarms with people. So today I savour the privilege of having the place all to myself and imagine what it might have been like to be the first one ever to leave wet footprints here.

The waves mark time like a natural metronome. The lightly spritzing rain and steady rhythm of the sea relax me, and I ease into a walking meditation. I know I am not alone in the joy I get from being here. Over the years, wave after wave of people have arrived at Long Beach and been enchanted in the same way I have. They tackle the bumpy, winding, and often narrow road that crosses the mountainous spine of Vancouver Island, finally spilling out of their vehicles at Incinerator, where the forest at last parts to reward the new arrivals with a glimpse of the fabled beach. Children and dogs hit the sand running. Adults follow at a stroll, stretching, gazing up and down the beach and out to sea, tilting their faces back to breathe deeply the briny air.

If Long Beach had a historical and geographic heart, the beach near Incinerator would be it. Before the current highway and the rough dirt road that preceded it, a footpath near here connected the sheltered bay on the other side of the Esowista Peninsula to this wilder, surf-pounded shore. Anyone wanting to get to the exposed coast would land a canoe or small boat on the quiet mudflats in Grice Bay. From there, a trail across the peninsula to the open ocean delivered them here. Thus, for thousands of years, this place was the primary access point to the exposed coast at the Tofino end of the peninsula. And while access options may have changed over the past century, Incinerator remains the place where many people get their first real glimpse of Long Beach.

One might think that the name Incinerator is an imaginative reference to how the powerful force of barrelling waves might "burn up" unwary swimmers and surfers. Certainly that's a more evocative image than the reality—which is that during World War II a large incinerator was installed here to burn garbage from a nearby military base.

Today, Long Beach is part of Pacific Rim National Park Reserve. Creation of the park in the 1970s brought a good sample of the Pacific Coast ecosystem into Canada's national park system. With a boundary extending seaward to a depth of 10 fathoms, Pacific Rim also became the country's first national park with a marine component. Although Long Beach's iconic stretch of sand is the main draw for the park's 800,000 annual visitors, no less interesting is the area's biodiversity and natural abundance.

In the intertidal zone, where sea and land mingle twice daily, living tapestries of algae and invertebrates entwine. In the temperate rainforests, myriad layers of green vegetation compete and coexist with equal measure in thick, damp lushness. In the squelching bogs and the xeric (dry) sand dunes, Lilliputian plants hold their own against the elements. And in the slick, pudding-like mud of the park's tidal flats, invertebrates—worms, shrimp, clams, and more—thrive, as do the birds that love them. Grey whales and silver salmon, wolves and cougars, red-billed oystercatchers and rufous hummingbirds, sea stars and sand dollars, banana slugs and their dromedary jumping-slug cousins—all of these creatures and many others populate and feed the Long Beach area's web of life.

No less varied and rich has been the area's human history. Like the flood tides rising across Long Beach's shores daily, people have swept into the area in distinct waves: First Peoples for millennia, followed in recent times by explorers and settlers, miners and loggers, dreamers and schemers, airmen and artists, hippies and surfers, and, in more recent times, tourists. Not only

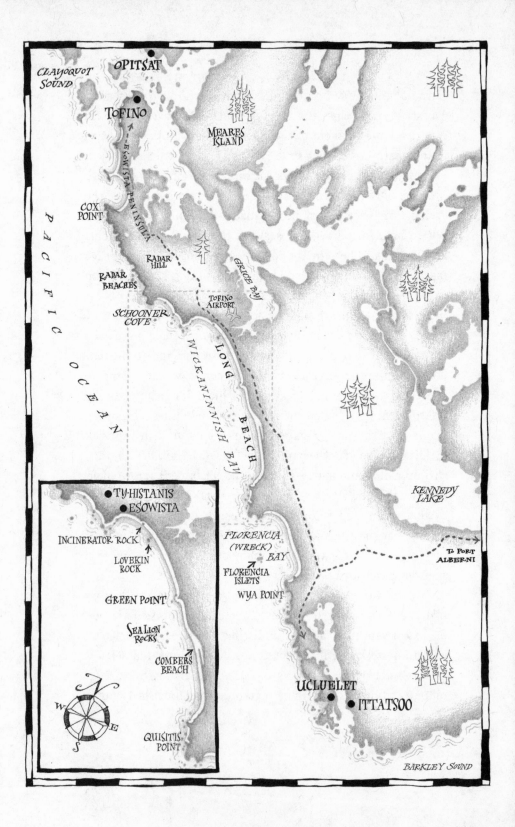

were their lives uniquely supported and shaped by the nature of this wild coastal world, but in turn a lot of what they did left a mark on sand, sea, and land. Even the sober reality of rain (about four metres, or thirteen feet, annually) and thrashing winter storms has never, it seems, been able to dampen the resolve of the people drawn to live in this place. The unvarnished vigour of this land-sea edge has always held an allure.

THIS BOOK focuses on what I call the "Greater Long Beach Area," essentially from Cox Point to Wya Point and across the peninsula to Grice Bay. It also touches on the histories of Tofino, Ucluelet, Clayoquot and Barkley Sounds, and other island areas, for events there dictated events at Long Beach. The straight-line distance from Cox to Wya Points is about twenty-four kilometres (fifteen miles), but if one were to walk the shoreline, that distance would stretch to almost thirty-five kilometres (twenty-two miles) along a series of beaches interrupted by rocky headlands. Long Beach proper fringes Wickaninnish Bay and extends from Portland Point to near the national park's interpretive centre, a distance of almost sixteen kilometres (ten miles). The beach at Florencia Bay (also called Wreck Bay) adds about five kilometres (three miles) more. (See map on facing page.)

While the actual size of this area may seem small, looming large are the people who, literally or figuratively, rode in on flood tides and stayed awhile to live, work, or play. By no means have I tried to provide a definitive history of the area—the tales of shipwrecks alone could make a doorstop of a book. Rather, my hope is that the sample of stories and natural history details I've included here will illuminate both the area's physical setting and the notable human dramas that have unfolded against its backdrop.

signatures in soil
and stone

IT IS a cool morning in early spring, and I'm down on Florencia Bay. Word is quietly spreading in town that glass balls—hollow glass floats once used on Japanese fishing nets—have been washing in on local beaches. I suspect I've arrived too late to find one. The die-hard hunters will have been out long before sunrise, some sporting headlamps and conducting their search on bikes.

Glass float treasures or not, I take beach walks for the sheer mind-and-body pleasure of it. On this day, only a few other people are around. They slip into view and fade out again, veiled in the morning's soft mist. I look for bits of beach glass, weathered shards of glass in teal green or beer-bottle brown, whose surfaces have been frosted and edges smoothed by years of tumbling

7

in water and sand. When it comes to gifts from the sea, I am easy to please. A prize bit of beach glass or an unusual rock (preferably with a good story attached) will do every time.

Jack Martin appreciated unusual rocks, too. Martin and his wife, Phyllis, lived at Long Beach in the 1960s right up until the national park was established. Their house, built just above the beach, was known for its hand-hewn timbers, portholes, and a wall of floor-to-ceiling plate-glass windows with half-inch thick panes that Jack had salvaged from an old Seattle hotel.

While they were still in the process of building the house, Jack took a fancy to a concretion on the beach at Florencia Bay. The naturally formed and perfectly rounded sandstone ball with its pockmarked surface was so big that an adult could not encircle it with both arms. To residents of the area, the "meteorite" was a well-known feature at the bay.

Martin thought this notable rock would look nice in his yard. Once, when Phyllis was away on a trip, he went to work with an excavator, cutting a rough road down to the beach. There, he scooped up the rock, transported it back up the hill, and proudly positioned it at the end of his driveway. When Phyllis returned a few weeks later, she was not impressed that their home had gained a "moon rock" but still lacked windows.

After the national park came into being, the concretion was retrieved and installed briefly at the naturalist's office before again being moved to the top of the cliffs above Florencia Bay for everyone to see and appreciate. There it might have stayed for many decades more, except that in January 2009 it was stolen and tipped off the bluff above Green Point. While the culprits showed a modicum of consideration (leaving money at the site during the heist, presumably to cover the cost of the two gate locks they cut to reach the rock), they never did come forward.

To this day, the details of the Great Concretion Heist—who, how, and why—remain unsolved.

The concretion's three journeys back and forth from Florencia Bay to Long Beach were, of course, only the most recent trips in its history. Concretions are hard balls of sandstone, created when sediments build up around a nucleus such as shell and ultimately become cemented together, forming a rock. This concretion may have first travelled to Florencia Bay packed into one of the great sheets of ice that covered North America tens of thousands of years ago. Here, it was part of the load of till dropped as the ice sheet melted, which is now exposed in the sandy cliffs rising above the bay. Over time, as the wind, rain, and waves scraped away the softer material from around this geological curiosity, the exposed concretion finally fell out of the cliff to the beach below. There it may have stayed but for the intervention of a man and his excavator.

Foundations

Two hundred million years ago, Long Beach didn't exist. Nor did the land mass occupied today by British Columbia. Back then, the edge of the North American continent was close to what is now the British Columbia–Alberta border. Just as most of the people who come to Long Beach are visitors from other regions, the rock here is also "from away." Much of British Columbia is a mélange of sorts, a mish-mash of sedimentary, igneous, and metamorphic rocks that originated in distant latitudes.

The province's geological underpinnings are linked to the activities of the tectonic plates, the great slabs of Earth's lithosphere (outer layer) that fit together like pieces of a jigsaw puzzle. Sediments have always run off the continent, flushed by rain and carried by rivers to the sea. As the oceanic plate subducts

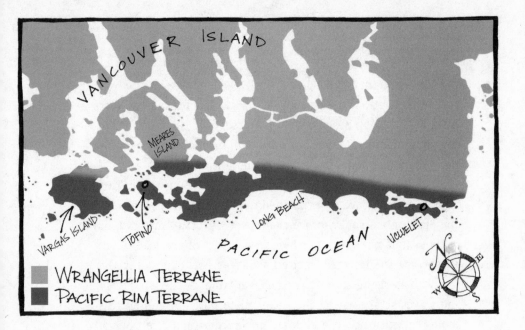

WRANGELLIA TERRANE
PACIFIC RIM TERRANE

Like a patchwork quilt, British Columbia is a colourful geological aggregate of exotic terranes, each with its own origin and composition. Long Beach is part of the Pacific Rim Terrane.

beneath the continent, the action scrapes these accumulated sediments off the sea floor, fusing them to the plates' leading edges. Any volcanic islands carried atop the oceanic plates also become joined to the continental plates in this way. Each island and slab of rock "accreted" onto the continent is called a terrane.

About 100 million years ago, a chain of volcanic islands collided with the ancient edge of the continent. This terrane of exotic rock, called Wrangellia, forms much of Vancouver Island as well as Haida Gwaii (the Queen Charlotte Islands) and parts of British Columbia's mainland.

The rock under Long Beach, however, is different from that which formed the rest of Wrangellia. The section of the coast between Tofino and Ucluelet is part of the Pacific Rim Terrane, which adhered to Wrangellia about 55 million years ago. It's a sliver of a terrane, snuggled up to Vancouver Island only on the Ucluelet–Long Beach–Tofino stretch, on the outer edge of Vargas Island, and down near Port Renfrew and Victoria. The Pacific Rim Terrane is a mélange of the sand, gravel, silt, limestone, and volcanic rocks deposited on the ocean floor between 150 and 200 million years ago. All of these are visible in the twisted, buckled rocks of the outcrops along the west coast shoreline.

Nature's Sculpting

About seventeen thousand years ago, at the height of the last ice age, only the highest mountains on Vancouver Island would have poked above the thick cap of ice. Today these peaks are jagged and sharp, noticeably different from the lower mountains near Long Beach that were smoothed over by ice, such as Vargas Cone and Radar Hill.

As the ice first expanded and then receded, it sculpted the landscape into the forms visible throughout the area today. Deep gouging carved the narrow, snaking fjords of Clayoquot Sound and Alberni Inlet. These were further shaped by the erosive forces of water flowing down the river valleys. The retreating ice also left behind mountainous loads of glacial till, a mixture of mud, clay, sand, gravel, and pebbles. At Long Beach, these large-scale "till drops" can be seen in the towering sand cliffs, studded with stones like raisins in a baked cake, that rise above sections of Florencia and Wickaninnish Bays. Over thousands of years, waves and winds sorted the till so that today we have the extensive mudflats on one side of the Esowista Peninsula and the series of sandy beaches on the outer coast.

The Long Beach area is part of the Estevan Lowland, a narrow strip of shoreline that stretches about 290 kilometres (180 miles) along Vancouver Island's southwest coast. In most locations, the lowland is less than 3 kilometres (2 miles) wide and has few dramatic topographical features or landmarks. Nevertheless, the area's stunning beaches—really, more like one stunning beach punctuated by rocky headlands and stretching almost from Tofino to Ucluelet—seems a fair trade for the subdued landscape.

Sand extending far back into the forests above many local beaches also reveals the history of the ice age on this coast. The height and shape of the shoreline have changed over time in response to changes in sea level and to the rise and fall of the island's land mass. Most recently, as the kilometres-thick ice melted and drained into the ocean, the sea level rose. So, too, did the unburdened land lift, gradually rising as its frozen mantle got smaller and finally disappeared.

At one site not far from Long Beach, archaeologists have determined that sea levels during the Holocene Epoch (which began about 12,000 years ago) were at least 10 metres (30 feet) below where they are today. Then, from about 6,000 to 4,800 years ago, sea levels rose to about 3 to 4 metres (10 to 13 feet) *above* the existing shoreline before falling again to present-day levels. Further proof of this constant flux and recalibrating of sea level over time is evident at the base of Radar Hill, just northwest of Long Beach. There, evidence of an old shoreline shows that sea level was once 15 metres (50 feet) higher than it is today.

This extremely slow, non-stop adjustment of land continues. By this time next year, the west coast of Vancouver Island will have risen by about one millimetre, while the whole of the island will have been nudged about a centimetre northward.

Much of the land near Long Beach is a low coastal plain. Expansive mudflats predominate in the calm, inner waters sheltered by the Esowista Peninsula. Sand and cobble beaches are found on the outer, exposed, and "high-energy" shorelines.

When the Earth Moves

The west coast of Vancouver Island is the most seismically active place in Canada. Every once in a while, earthquakes and tremors near or far remind us that living on a low coastal plain exposes us to all the whims of the Pacific Rim's tectonic restlessness. Tsunami warnings and earthquake preparedness are the stuff of our lives.

This was the case on March 11, 2011, when a magnitude 9.0 earthquake rocked eastern Japan. Within hours, all of the Long Beach area's communities were officially on tsunami watch. The Provincial Emergency Program called the warning, as did officials in other countries rimming the Pacific. West coast communities had not been so alert to an earthquake and tsunami

THE QUAKE OF 1865

On August 25, 1865, William Torrens and a small group of men surveying Clayoquot Sound for minerals experienced a sizeable quake. Torrens wrote, "About 9 pm we felt a tremendous earthquake—the first shock lasted for two minutes and created an oscillation exactly such as one has felt when travelling at full speed in an Express Railway train." Two minor shocks followed. The next day, the men had to pick their way through hundreds of uprooted trees.

In an appendix to his report to the governor of the Colony of Vancouver Island, Torrens wrote about "Indian Superstitions," including native reaction to the earthquake. By his account, the native people interpreted the earthquake as the heavy footfalls of an evil spirit coming to Earth to "slay the living for the evil they have committed." Torrens scoffed at this interpretation: "We laughed at their superstition and explained to them as best we could how Earthquakes really occur."

For all his assuredness, Torrens's explanation was wrong. He attributed the earthquake to expansion of the earth's crust, an accepted theory of the time. Thanks to plate tectonics being fully explained in the 1960s, we now know otherwise.

warning for years. Park beaches were closed, as was the high school in Ucluelet because school buses delivering students from Tofino would have been passing Long Beach close to the time of any expected waves. The waves never did arrive, and the only impact detected was unusually strong currents in the harbours. However, even a small wave generated by the quake could have made an impact on such a low-lying peninsula—essentially a flat plain with an average elevation of less than twenty-five metres (eighty-two feet). In an area where many people live *at* sea level, even a rise of a foot or two is worth paying attention to, particularly if the tsunami occurs at high tide.

In recent memory we've been spared an assault by a monster tsunami but, as geologists and the odds tell us, we're in line for a big wave or two. Oral histories and geological clues tell us they have hit before.

LIVING ON RESTLESS SHORES

Not far offshore from Long Beach is the point where two tectonic plates converge. The denser Juan de Fuca plate sits lower, covered by ocean, and the North American continental plate floats like a giant raft. These two plates meet at the Cascadia Subduction Zone, where the Juan de Fuca plate is forced downward, subducting beneath the continental plate, sliding under it at an annual rate of two to five centimetres (one to two inches).

Although in this area we experience many low-magnitude earthquakes caused by complex forces acting within the crustal plates, the much more catastrophic events are earthquakes that deform the crust. These happen when the plates lock together. Tremendous pressure builds until the plates abruptly unlock, causing the crust to jerk upward. Such "megathrust" earthquakes occur only along subduction zones, just like the one off the west coast of Vancouver Island. They are the strongest earthquakes in the world, striking every three hundred to eight hundred years or so. A 1964 earthquake in Alaska was the largest recorded in North America, with a magnitude of 9.2. Even larger was the Chilean earthquake of 1960, which, at magnitude 9.5, remains the largest earthquake ever recorded.

Two earthquakes strong enough to make the list of Canada's top ten earthquakes in the last century have rocked the Long

Beach region. On December 6, 1918, a magnitude 7 earthquake shook Mike Hamilton awake. He was north of Long Beach, at Ahousat on Flores Island, helping build a school for the Presbyterian Church. The work crew slept in the partially completed building. When the quake struck at 12:41 A.M., the men waited in terror as the structure rattled, fully expecting to be crushed in their beds. At nearby Hesquiat, missionary Father Charles Moser recorded the same event in his diary: "I thought the end of the world was here."

Three decades later, on June 23, 1946, a magnitude 7.3 earthquake shook the Vancouver Island town of Courtenay. In communities closest to the epicentre, 75 percent of homes lost their chimneys. Up the coast from Long Beach, at Estevan Light, lighthouse keepers scrambled to cope with chaos. At the time, the lighthouse lens floated upon a vat of mercury. News accounts reported that the quake jarred several of the lens prisms loose and knocked more than four hundred kilograms (nine hundred pounds) of mercury out of the bath. One can only imagine what it took to contain quivery blobs of that much toxic mercury rolling around the tower's floors like ball bearings. As far away as Victoria water mains broke, buildings were damaged, and the recording mechanism on the city's seismograph (an instrument for measuring earthquakes) dislodged. Nearer to Long Beach, the captain of the MV *Uchuck,* plying the Alberni Canal, experienced a series of "long, gently-sinusoidal swells" that were so out of the ordinary he thought the engine's tail shaft was broken.

THE GREATEST WAVE

The sinusoidal waves the *Uchuck* surfed down were the ocean's response to the earthquake. When tectonic plates shift, sometimes dropping a metre or more in seconds, the water above the seabed shifts to fill the void. This rapid movement of such a colossal amount of water produces a tsunami, or earthquake-generated wave (often erroneously called a "tidal wave"). Depending on where the waves are initiated and in which direction they move, the result can vary from a negligible rise that only the finest of instruments can detect to a devastating surge like the Indian Ocean tsunami that struck on Boxing Day 2004.

Over three hundred years ago, on January 26, 1700, Canada's west coast experienced a catastrophic earthquake at the Cascadia Subduction Zone. The quake and its tandem wave of destruction are preserved in both the oral history and geological record of the area. According to stories told through generations, Chief Louie Clamhouse of the Huu-ay-aht First Nation recounted the devastation that the 1700 quake wrought at Pachena Bay, just down the coast from Long Beach:

> It was at nighttime that the land shook... [People] simply had no time to get hold of canoes, no time to get awake... It is said no one ever knew what happened. I think a big wave smashed into the beach. The Pachena Bay people were lost.

The tidal flats near Long Beach provide their own record of that quake's tsunami. When abrupt changes in sea level occur and large wave events result, they leave a "signature" in the sand and soil sediments. The powerful surge of water floods the land with a slurry of seawater, mud, sand, and debris. These deposits trap pollen and other plant and animal remains, which scientists analyze to find out the approximate date for the change in the soil profile. Studies like this conducted in the mudflats near Tofino show evidence of a tsunami about three hundred years ago—evidence that fits with the oral history of the Huu-ay-aht people, as well as with written accounts from Japan of a tsunami striking at several sites along its coast on January 27, 1700.

THE TSUNAMI OF 1964

On Good Friday 1964, a magnitude 9.2 earthquake occurred 120 kilometres (75 miles) east of Anchorage, Alaska. Deep below the earth's surface, the North American plate suddenly detached from the oceanic Pacific plate and lurched seaward, setting everything above it into a rattling frenzy for 4 minutes. The sudden motion deformed the crust, uplifting some sections as high as 9 metres (30 feet) and generating a prodigious tsunami that swept across the Pacific Ocean at velocities reaching 830 kilometres (515 miles) per hour, as fast as a commercial jet. Within 16 hours it had reached Antarctica. The tsunami killed 119 people, including 12 as far south from Alaska as Crescent City, California.

Geography dictated how the tsunami acted on Vancouver Island's west coast when it arrived less than 5 hours after the quake. When the giant open-ocean-fed swell of water arrived at Alberni Inlet, it ploughed in through the kilometre-wide opening and squeezed up the 40-kilometre- (25-mile-) long fjord, gathering size and momentum. Stopped in its tracks at the inlet's head, the debris-loaded wave surged into Port Alberni, knocking houses off their foundations, flipping cars, ripping boats from their moorings, and derailing a loaded freight train. More than 250 buildings were damaged, 60 extensively. Incredibly, no life was lost in the chaos of that night, but the clean-up was long, muddy, and expensive.

Although Port Alberni received most of the press coverage in British Columbia, other communities were affected by the tsunami, too. One was Hot Springs village in northern Clayoquot

Sound. In quick succession, three waves hit the village during the night. Several houses torn from their foundations floated into the bay and began to burn, ignited by tipped lanterns. Against a dark sky lit up by the flaming homes, residents clambered into boats and hurried from house to house ensuring everyone was safe, all the while negotiating whirlpools and bobbing stumps, logs, and other debris. No lives were lost there either, but damage was so great that the entire village was later relocated. In Tofino, the waves' ferocity left the municipal water line between the village and the water source on Meares Island twisted and broken on the mudflats. The anchors and chains securing village docks had been lifted and knocked askew. In Ucluelet, a log boom snapped apart, filling the inlet with logs that battered pilings out from under several wharfs. Townspeople remember the peculiar quiet that fell momentarily before each wave arrived and the roar that followed as the wall of water flooded past and over islets and smashed into the bays.

Out at Long Beach that night, resort owner Neil Buckle arrived home late after visiting his wife in hospital, where she had given birth to their first child. Awakened by crashing and rumbling, he looked out a window to see his Dodge truck awash in a tangle of logs and brush. By Neil's reckoning, the water flowed up Sandhill Creek beside the resort for well over a kilometre before pouring back down bearing logs, branches, and stumps. "I could see it in the moonlight," he recalled later. "The waves were as high as the room."

And So We Wait

Although dramatic and memorable, tsunamis that impart the damage of the 1964 earthquake are statistically rare. Of the forty-three tsunamis registered by the Tofino tide gauge

AN OCEAN OF INFLUENCE

The Pacific Ocean calls the water and weather shots out here. Long Beach's shores are like slates washed and blown clean every day. The sandy stretch you walked yesterday at noon might be covered in seawater the same time tomorrow. Each "swash line" (the band of sea-borne gifts delivered by the last incoming tide) is just a few hours old.

Any trip to the beach, especially for hiking or exploring the intertidal zone, requires spending time with a tide table beforehand. Every twelve hours at Long Beach, the tide moves from high to low and back again. This results in two high tides and two low tides daily. The time that the high and low tides occur, as well as their heights, is never the same two days in a row; a gradual cyclical change occurs throughout the year. In this region, the annual tidal range (that is, the range between the year's highest and lowest tides) is 4.1 metres (13.45 feet).

Some days, the Pacific sends in clear blue skies and gentle waves that *shoosh* up the beach, enticing children aged two to ninety-two to kick off their shoes and wade in. Other days, it turns the brutes loose— crashing rollers that arrive with a full surround-sound maelstrom of winds so relentless you need to struggle to hang onto your breath let alone your hat. And in between are the days the Pacific decides to mop out the heavens, leaving Long Beach under rains so heavy that no raingear, whatever the manufacturer's claim, is going to keep you dry.

The small chop generated by local winds is the common fare much of the year, but it's the big brassy breakers of the fall and winter that enthrall most people. They start as giant swells generated by storms far offshore and often travel for days before reaching Long Beach's shores. The longer a wave travels uninterrupted, the more energy it packs and the larger it is when it finally meets land. It is these large swells that keep surfers checking weather reports and the data provided by offshore buoys on swell height, direction, and distance between waves.

between 1906 and 1981, for example, only two resulted in waves higher than a metre. One was the 2.4-metre (7.9-foot) wave measured after Alaska's 1964 earthquake, and the other, a 1.26-metre (4.13-foot) wave, was recorded after the massive earthquake in Chile in 1960.

Still, earthquakes and tsunami risks come with the territory here. Threat of the "big one" looms in the background, but most residents don't dwell on it other than putting together (or thinking about putting together) a home earthquake kit. Local emergency preparedness crews have a more focused attitude about all of this, working hard to remind the rest of us of the shaky ground on which we live.

Imagine living in a place where the ground beneath your feet could shift and buckle at any moment, where the potential for a wave to sweep your home away is not just Hollywood fiction, and where geological reference points shift constantly, if infinitesimally, every day. Welcome to Long Beach. Life on the edge, indeed.

2

raincoast riches

A FAVOURITE SPOT of mine is a pocket beach just around a rocky headland from Long Beach itself. Its pitch is steep, not shallow like the big beach, and it is filled with pebbles and cobbles, not sand. While Long Beach has calm days among the tempestuous ones, this beach never seems to rest. Each time the surf rushes back down to the sea, it sets the stones knocking and clattering against each other in manic chatter. Barely does the din subside before the next set of incoming waves prompts a new chorus.

On warm days, my daughters and I have lain on this beach, using fat sun-roasted stones for our version of a hot-stone massage (kelp facials optional). Rainy days here are the best ones for combing through the masses of sea-buffed pebbles to admire

Nature's exquisite handiwork and seemingly boundless creativity in dreaming up colour and pattern combinations.

When the tide and waves allow—for this can also be a dangerous beach if one doesn't pay attention—I might climb one of the small columns of rock at the beach's north end. From here, I can see over to another high promontory where friends of ours were married one stormy winter day, fittingly clad in wet-weather gear and custom-painted rubber boots. That day, wisps of golden sea foam churned up by the sea and caught in the wind swirled around the couple in place of confetti.

This is also a good place to view the open ocean. It's not unusual to catch sight of grey whales on their yearly migration north from Baja California, Mexico, to the Arctic in the spring and then back south again in the fall.

Early native people living near here valued this site as well. This high point, with only one access, was a perfect lookout. It gave men a commanding view out to sea where they could watch not only for whales, an important food source for First Nations, but for canoes bearing neighbours, sometimes friend, sometimes foe.

The Coast's Ancient Cultures

Native people have called the Long Beach area home for millennia. An archaeological excavation at Ts'ishaa on Benson Island in the Broken Group Islands (today about a forty-five-minute boat ride from Ucluelet) calculated human settlement there as early as five thousand years ago. It hardly seems necessary, though, to pinpoint the exact beginnings of aboriginal history on the island's west coast. If human occupation was represented by a handful of beach pebbles, then the residency of non-native people would be but one or two of those small stones.

In a moist, humid climate like this, where wood was the primary building material, structures from the distant past do not survive as those of ancient civilizations in arid environments have. No pyramids here. Nonetheless, the history of Vancouver Island's First Nations—here since "time immemorial"—is recorded in rock carvings (called petroglyphs), shell middens, stone fishtraps, and moss-covered house posts. It also survives in the stories and memories passed down through more than two hundred generations and in the language of place names.

Today, the native people of Long Beach and elsewhere along Vancouver Island's west coast are collectively referred to as Nuu-chah-nulth, meaning people "all along the mountains and sea." The name Nuu-chah-nulth was chosen in 1979 by fourteen of the First Nations living on Vancouver Island west of the mountain range that forms the ragged spine of the island. Formerly they were called the Nootka, a name incorrectly applied when Captain James Cook arrived in 1778 and which stuck for almost two centuries.

While the Nuu-chah-nulth First Nations are connected through language, geography, and heredity, this collective name for all the residents of the west coast did not exist in the past. Instead, there were dozens of local groups made up of chiefs with territorial rights and privileges within specific areas. In the Long Beach area alone, at least six separate village sites existed between Cox and Wya Points. One was located at Green Point, the current site of the national park campground; another was at the south end of Wickaninnish Bay near the current site of the park's interpretive centre; and a third was at Esowista, which remains a First Nations village today.

As occurs within all political states, boundaries merged and shifted over time. Their composition also evolved, often

In the late 1890s, the British Columbia artist Emily Carr visited missionary friends at the First Nation village in Ucluelet Harbour. She sketched and painted the village's buildings and some of its inhabitants during her visit and later wrote that it was there she was given the name Klee Wyck (Laughing One).

influenced by warfare or marriage. For instance, where the community of Esowista sits today was once a village of the Hisawistaht (Esowistaht), whose territory covered parts of Long Beach across to Grice Bay. Following four years of battles with the Tla-o-qui-aht (events collectively referred to as the Great War), all of the Hisawistaht are thought to have died, after which the land was claimed by the Tla-o-qui-aht. Today, Esowista is translated as "clubbed to death."

Later, the effects of the Europeans' arrival also drove amalgamation. In face of the extreme destabilization this contact wrought on the coast's longstanding socio-political structures—made worse by plummeting population numbers resulting from previously unknown illnesses—many formerly independent groups banded together.

Today, there are two Nuu-chah-nulth nations whose traditional territories include lands in and around Long Beach. To the north are the Tla-o-qui-aht, whose name was anglicized to Clayoquot by early traders. Their territory encompasses much of the southern section of Clayoquot Sound, including the town site of Tofino, parts of Meares Island, the Kennedy Lake and Kennedy River areas, and part of Long Beach. Opitsat on Meares Island and Esowista at Long Beach are their primary villages today.

To the south, the Yuu-cluth-aht (Ucluelet) First Nation territory extends from Long Beach and around into Barkley Sound. The main village today is at Ittatsoo in Ucluelet Inlet.

A Life from Cedar and Sea

Come autumn, the paucity of deciduous trees on Vancouver Island makes the rainforest a little less colourful than other forests at comparable latitudes in Canada. Absent are the vibrant reds, yellows, and oranges of the eastern maples. Still, an October bike ride or walk along the Grice Bay Road reveals other forest treasures. The road here is lined with red alders whose leaves turn a mottled green and gold in the fall and look like ripple-cut potato chips. The upper branches arch overhead, giving the road a *grande allée* feel. Once the alders and salmonberry bushes drop their leaves, the forest behind them is exposed.

It was on one of my slower trips down the road that I first noticed a cedar tree with a four-metre- (thirteen-foot-) long strip of bark peeled away. The bottom of the strip scar was about a hand's width across, and the whole section tapered upward to a point. Farther along the road, I spotted two more cedars marked this way and then others as I continued on. These were recent "culturally modified trees," whose bark had been stripped by twenty-first-century Nuu-chah-nulth weavers carrying forward a traditional skill that has helped sustain First Nations culture on the west coast.

Along the trail to Halfmoon Bay is another, much older bark-stripped tree, a huge western redcedar. The scar is worn and greying now, but one spring, decades (or perhaps centuries) ago, a native woman approached this tree and addressed its spirit, thanking it for the valuable resource it was about to provide. She then used a knife of sharpened stone or shell to make a horizontal slice about a foot wide through the thick bark. Next, grasping the bark, she peeled the strip upward until it pulled away at the top. She folded the long strip in a bundle and strapped it on her back to carry home. There, she separated the soft inner bark from the rougher outer bark, ready to use in creating any one of dozens of items.

Traditional skills and knowledge of the uses of redcedar are still passed on through generations of Nuu-chah-nulth people. Redcedar is harvested today near Long Beach by Nuu-chah-nulth weavers. Gisele Martin learned the art of cedar bark harvesting from her aunt, Mary Martin.

LAND AND SHORE OF PLENTY

The western redcedar is sometimes referred to as the tree of life; virtually no other natural resource had so many uses for the region's first inhabitants. Easy to split, naturally resistant to rot, and aromatic, the bark and wood of the redcedar (and of the yellow-cedar) lent themselves to a comprehensive list of applications, including building construction, clothing, fishing and hunting gear, transportation, burial needs, and the arts. Waterproof capes, hats, mats, and baskets were woven from long strips of the pliable inner bark. Shelters, ranging from enormous multi-family houses to small temporary structures, were constructed from cedar posts, beams, and planks. Canoes—from small, shallow crafts that a woman might use in calm waters to gather clover roots to whaling vessels that could hold crews of eight men—were carved from single cedar trunks. Watertight containers used for storage and cooking were fashioned from thin slabs of cedar that were steamed, scored, and bent into boxes. From the everyday to the extraordinary, the cedar tree provided so much.

Bark harvesting traditionally happened in the spring when the sap was flowing. Although they had larger, permanent village sites, native people moved throughout their territory as the natural resources they relied on came into season. In February, the Herring Spawn Moon marked the end of winter. The Nuu-chah-nulth moved from their winter villages to fishing stations where great schools of herring swam close to shore to spawn. Using large rakes, people scooped herring from the water and dried them for later use. They also strung hemlock boughs or fronds of giant kelp in the water to catch the sticky spawn.

Spring was also when the year's fresh greens, such as the new shoots of the salmonberry bush, were harvested. In early summer, the fat orange-red salmonberries added vitamin C and some sweetness to people's diets. Other edible berries ripened successively through the year: thimbleberry, red huckleberry, blueberry, cynamocka (evergreen huckleberry), and salal.

From the time that creamy-white herring milt clouded coastal waters in the spring to the day the last slab of salmon was dried and stored late in the fall, the Yuu-cluth-aht and Tla-o-qui-aht people crisscrossed their territories, harvesting, fishing, and hunting for the food that fulfilled their immediate and wintertime needs. Some harvesting sites were located on and near Long Beach. Plants for food, medicine, and other uses were gathered from the forests fringing the shoreline. Seafood,

GIFTS OF THE SALMON

On the west coast, salmon—chinook, coho, sockeye, pink, and chum (also called dog)—are the threads that stitch together land, rivers, and sea. Their lives begin in fresh water, where eggs laid in the gravel hatch into fry, and continue on from there through briny estuaries and down into the sea. Years later, adult salmon nearing the end of their lives make the return journey to their natal streams, guided largely by their astonishing sense of smell. There, they lay or fertilize the next generation of eggs before dying.

Like cedar, salmon has always been important to First Nations on the west coast. Trolling for salmon was done in most months of the year. During the spawning season, which extends from the late summer runs of sockeye and pink to the dark days of November when the last of the coho return to their streams, people were kept busy harvesting and preserving the fish for use throughout the year.

Salmon's gifts benefit the ecology of the entire region. Live salmon, at various life stages, are prey for many other animals, from trout and American dippers, which eat the eggs, to killer whales and bears, which eat the adult fish. Even in death, salmon sustain life. Dozens of animal species gorge on the salmon carcasses that fill the streams in the fall. Recent studies have shown how the dead fish, when dragged into the woods by bears, provide a primary source of nitrogen fertilizer for the forest habitat.

including razor clams, urchins, chitons, snails, and crabs, was abundant along the beach, on rocky outcrops and in tidal pools. Salmon trolling was good near shore, particularly around small islets and rocky headlands like those at Gowlland Rocks or Box Island in Schooner Cove. Halibut, seals, sea lions, and rockfish all were harvested within sight of Long Beach and its associated villages. Hunted whales were brought ashore to protected areas of the beach, and lookouts were ever vigilant for drift whales, a much-valued natural gift from the sea. (One of the battles in the Hisawistaht–Tla-o-qui-aht war was instigated by an argument over who had the rights to a drift whale that had come ashore.)

Across the peninsula, the waters of Grice Bay provided access to interior salmon streams as well as to great flocks of shorebirds and waterfowl that dwelt in the mudflat habitat.

While the Nuu-chah-nulth harvested a bounty of resources from the forest and foreshore, they were also a highly maritime culture, travelling great distances by canoe, often on the open ocean, to trade with and visit others and, perhaps most famously, to hunt whales.

THE WHALERS

All First Nations within Nuu-chah-nulth territory are traditionally nations of whalers. The expedition to intercept, kill, and tow home a whale from a canoe on the open ocean was as pivotal an annual harvesting event as it was perilous.

Preparation began during the winter, when the Nuu-chah-nulth stayed close to their main village sites, living off stored food and whatever the occasional hunting or fishing foray turned up. Much of this time was spent carving and repairing canoes and paddles, twining long lengths of cedar and sinew into rope, and crafting the all-important harpoons.

Before Europeans brought iron to the coast, hunters made harpoon tips from the shells of large mussels (now called California mussels, these can be longer than a human hand). These were bound with sinew and cemented with spruce gum to a two-part spearhead made of bone or elk antler. It seems inconceivable that mussel shell could be sharp enough to pierce the leathery hide of a whale, but each shell was carefully and precisely ground with sharpening stones to a near-razor-thin edge.

The next step was to prepare the crew and their families. Among the Nuu-chah-nulth, there were few honours higher than being chosen "the whaler," the man who led the hunt and threw the first harpoon. Needing great physical strength and agility, ambitious young men often turned to supernatural aid—prayer, fasting, and other rituals—to gain the power necessary to become a great whaler. Such exacting preparation was essential: these men were hunting animals longer than a transit bus and as massive as six male African elephants.

Once materially, physically, and spiritually ready, the hunters embarked on the mission, with several canoes travelling together to share the dangerous work. Far out on the water, they watched for the telltale spouts of their prey, usually humpback whales. Once a whale was spotted, the hunters moved into position. The lead canoe moved to the left side of the whale so that the whaler could plunge in the harpoon near the left pectoral fin when the animal rose for a breath. If the hit was on target, the men in the stern quickly manoeuvred the canoe away from the whale's thrashing tail, while the men in the bow released lines to which inflated sealskin floats were attached. When the whale rose again, another harpoon was thrown, tied with more line and floats. As the whale tired, the canoe moved in closer and the crew threw lances to finish the job. The final task was for one of the crew to

GREYS ON PARADE

Each spring around mid-March, Long Beach–area residents celebrate the return of the grey whales with the annual Pacific Rim Whale Festival. The opening day parade is a big draw for children—there seem to be more kids *in* the parade than watching it.

Launching the two-week-long party with a parade is appropriate, as the whales appear in a sort of parade, too. Their migration begins early in the year, when the first animals swim out of their breeding and calving grounds in the shallow, salty lagoons of Mexico's Baja peninsula. From there, the mammals follow their internal compasses, turning right and heading north, staying close to the coast. Thousands of the whales (some estimates say 24,000) eventually reach the Bering and Chukchi Seas. There, they feast for the summer on shrimp-like invertebrates, fishes, worms, and other small organisms they can strain from the water, often gorging more than 450 kilograms (990 pounds) a day. Around mid-October, the whales, with their bodies' fat stores renewed after months of feasting, begin their return trip south.

Grey whales, smaller than their humpback relations, are the most common species in the Long Beach area today. They weren't always, though. Humpbacks were once just as plentiful and are thought to be the species preferred by Nuu-chah-nulth whalers. Their numbers are slowly increasing from their near annihilation during the commercial whaling era, and nowadays whale watchers are often treated to their acrobatics off the coast.

Grey whales use their short baleen (flexible, fringed "plates" rooted in the palate) to strain food from the water. These whales are unique, however, because they are the only baleen whale known to feed on the ocean floor. To do this, a grey whale rolls onto its side, lays its head on the sea bottom, and, like a vacuum cleaner, sucks up huge amounts of water and sediment. Then, aided by the action of its 1,100-kilogram (2,425-pound) tongue, it sieves the water, mud, and sand out through the baleen, which leaves behind amphipods, tube worms, and other small organisms.

Through the work of Jim Darling and others, it is now known that certain whales always return to the Long Beach area and that some stay throughout the year.

Their propensity for shallow coastal waters makes greys one of the most watched whale species today. It was once thought that all the whales just passed by Long Beach during their migration. (The first ecotour operations on the west coast didn't advertise whales in their brochures because they thought sightings would be unreliable.) This idea began to change in the mid-1970s, when Jim Darling, a surfer, sea lion tour guide, and later naturalist for the national park, noticed that in the height of summer, and sometimes even in the winter, he often shared the waters off Long Beach with grey whales. This shattered the myth that all the whales completed the entire migration from Mexico to the Arctic. Clearly, some were hanging around Long Beach. Darling was so interested in the matter that he went on to study grey whales, eventually earning his PhD and becoming an authority on grey and humpback whales in the northeastern Pacific. Two of the whales he photographed in those early years, Two Dot Star and Saddle, were still alive and visiting the waters near Long Beach as of 2010.

dive into the water and sew the whale's mouth shut to prevent the body from filling with water and sinking as it was towed to shore.

Butchering the animal was as infused with ritual as the preparation before the hunt. Meat was divided among the crew and villagers according to a strict protocol. The blubber was boiled in wooden boxes and the oil skimmed off and stored in bags made from whale stomachs and bladders. The cooked blubber, as well as the flesh of the whale, was sun-dried or smoked and stored for later consumption. Sinew, bone, and baleen were also used.

A successful hunt topped up larders, but for the Nuu-chah-nulth, the very act meant so much more. Whaling was also about culture, social organization, and tradition.

A Resilient People

For at least half of the ten thousand years it has taken the coastal rainforest to evolve into its current state, the forests and waters of the Long Beach area have supported a human population. Those who have survived and thrived through the cycles of ecological change, not to mention through the much shorter but much more devastating contact with Europeans, are a testament to perseverance and the ability to adapt as the world around them has changed.

Native people were the first residents and stewards here. Today, they are still writing their stories on Long Beach forests and shores.

FOLLOWING PAGE: Often referred to as Lismer Beach (after artist Arthur Lismer), this cove was the location of one of several First Nations villages on Long Beach.

3

on the map

THE OBSERVATION deck of the national park's interpretive centre is the perfect place to take in a panoramic view of Long Beach. Along the sandy sweep that stretches out to my right, long ridges of waves rise up momentarily before spilling over gracefully in a tangle of froth-tipped curls. To my left, the sea swirls in over foreshore rocks that are both slick with algae and crusty with barnacles. A pair of red-billed oystercatchers circle the nearby islets, their long bright beaks providing brief stitches of colour across the flat grey sky. Their squeaky-toy *ratta-tatta-tat* calls pierce the sea's steady thrum.

This view would have been virtually the same for other people in other times—250, 500, and even 1,000 years ago—standing where I am now. That said, there is at least one key

Giant kelp and bull kelp create ecologically rich underwater forests that are home to myriad creatures, from fish to invertebrates and even marine mammals. The rope-like stalks, called stipes, can grow to thirty metres (ninety-eight feet) long.

difference. In the past, massive beds of kelp swayed in the water just off the rocks below, their golden-brown fronds streaming out like silky tresses.

Kelp is still visible along the shore today. However, this growth is like comparing a tiny woodlot to the expansive "forests" of kelp that flourished here and off rocky headlands all along the west coast before the Europeans arrived. The reason for kelp's decline is closely tied to the near-total expunging of one of this shoreline's most iconic and ecologically important inhabitants, the sea otter.

While the first Europeans may have come to the northwest coast of North America initially to claim lands for their country or to look for a shortcut to Asia, it was the sea otter that turned their heads and kept them coming back. This chance intersection of the west coast's indigenous people, European explorers and traders, and the sea otter set off a series of events that would forever alter both the history of coastal peoples and the ecology of the ocean from which they lived.

The Europeans Arrive

Despite the flurry of traffic on the west coast in the late eighteenth and early nineteenth centuries, an area like Long Beach held little particular interest. The protected sounds bookending the beach were a much greater draw to mariners, providing safe anchorages, freshwater sources, and ready access to native people for trading business. Although the Spaniards under Juan Pérez first made contact and traded briefly with native people off the coast of Vancouver Island in July 1774, it was the voyage of British Captain James Cook four years later that lit the fuse of change in this corner of the world.

Cook sailed in with two ships, the *Resolution* and the *Discovery*, while searching for a northern route between Europe and Asia. He made landfall at a harbour he called King George's Sound (later named Nootka Sound) where the native people (today known as the Mowachaht) guided Cook and his crews through the fog to an anchorage near their village, Yuquot. There, the visitors remained for most of April 1778, repairing their ships, surveying the area, and trading knives, chisels, nails, buttons, and other items with the Nuu-chah-nulth in exchange for fur and fresh food. While the trip was notable in that it was the first time the two cultures spent time together, it might have been of little consequence but for one trade item in particular: the three hundred or so sea otter pelts acquired by the British.

If nothing else, the crew surmised, the furs would keep them warm on the Arctic leg of their journey. Some sailors even used them as bedding. It was only when they got to China, where

A POPULOUS PLACE

Early journals by Cook and other explorers provide an invaluable account of Nuu-chah-nulth life at the beginning of sustained contact with Europeans. Of particular interest are references to the large populations the area supported. In 1788, for instance, John Meares wrote of visiting the longhouse of Chief Wickaninnish at Echachist in Clayoquot Sound and seeing eight hundred people gathered in the building. Chiefs Maquinna and Wickaninnish—whose names and titles have been passed down through the generations—were both frequently mentioned in the journals of early fur traders.

In 1791, when two vessels from the Spanish Navy arrived in Clayoquot Sound, fifty-eight canoes paddled out from the village to greet them. Commander Eliza wrote that the Tla-o-qui-aht people had five large settlements in southern Clayoquot Sound, each with about fifteen hundred inhabitants.

the furs fetched up to $120 apiece—a princely sum for the era—that the crew realized the astounding profit afforded by the pelts. Suddenly, the northeast Pacific was eyed with fresh interest. Wrote the *Resolution*'s acting captain, James King (for Cook had lost his life in Hawaii en route to China in 1779): "The rage with which our seamen were possessed to return . . . and, with another cargo of skins to make their fortunes, was not far short of mutiny."

Although the crew did not get their wish when the ships were directed back to England, news of this lucrative new commercial enterprise quickly inspired plans for future journeys to this part of the world. Cook's journals were published in 1784 and sold out in three days. Five more printings followed in rapid succession, and translated versions began to appear elsewhere in Europe. Within a few years, the west coast of Vancouver Island was teeming with merchant vessels engaged in trade for sea otter pelts.

Otter Pelt Bonanza

The first British ship to scoot back, the unapologetically named *Sea Otter* under the command of James Hanna, arrived at Nootka on August 18, 1785. In short order, the crew accumulated 560 sea otter pelts. The opening bell of the sea otter pelt trade had been rung. At least 170 ships eventually followed Hanna's. The British, who the native people called the King George Men, kept Nootka Sound as their base of operations. The Americans, called the Boston Men, established theirs in Clayoquot Sound to the south.

This booming trade was amicable on both sides for the most part. There were notable and tragic exceptions, such as the American destruction of the village of Opitsat by cannon fire in 1792, which led to reprisals from the Nuu-chah-nulth. Generally, however, it was a reciprocal business arrangement in which native people hunted the sea otters in exchange for a variety of goods. Chief Maquinna at Nootka Sound, Chief Wickaninnish in Clayoquot Sound, and others were savvy traders and readily became key players in the exchange. Because they controlled trade in their respective territories, the chiefs were able to regulate supply and demand by acting as middlemen between their neighbours and the trading ships. Their power and authority in the region grew as a result.

This stretch of coastline, including Long Beach, stayed the focus of the international maritime fur trade until the 1820s. By that point, after just over 50 years, the sea otter population had

THE COMPLICATIONS OF REINTRODUCTION

Between 1969 and 1972, efforts to reintroduce the sea otter to the west coast began in Kyuquot Sound, about 175 kilometres (109 miles) north of Long Beach. The initiative was successful, and today the population is slowly re-establishing up and down Vancouver Island's west coast. While this may sound like a good-news story, complete with a charming animal at its centre, not everyone is welcoming the sea otter's return. For almost 200 years, the sea otters haven't been here looking for their share of food. Now they're back, and they're hungry—and that means competition with other animals and humans for some of the same resources.

Sea otters are the only species of marine mammal without blubber. Their luxurious 2-layered fur is their ticket to survival in the cold waters of the northern Pacific. On an adult male, the dense underfur can have up to 800 million fibres. (In contrast, the average human head has 100,000 hairs.) When fluffed with air, this layer provides insulation from the cold. Food helps keep the animals warm, too. Otters have a high metabolism. To keep their internal furnaces stoked, they must eat up to a third of their body weight every day. Their diet is like a seafood smorgasbord that includes clams, crabs, snails, and—key to this story—sea urchins.

Sea urchins are herbivores that graze on kelp and other algae. Before the maritime fur trade, sea otters kept the spiky marine mowers in check. When the otter population collapsed, however, the urchins lost their major predator. Soon, they had chewed their way through the kelp, reducing the once-huge underwater forests to small fragmented remnants. In turn, the loss of these kelp forests dramatically changed the near-shore marine ecology. The two main species in these forests, giant kelp and bull kelp, can grow to such heights that they create a three-dimensional habitat in the ocean close to the shoreline. Kelp forests provide shelter and breeding habitat for many species of fish, including salmon, perch, greenling, and lingcod, and for dozens of invertebrates, from worms and brittle stars that entangle themselves in the kelp's root-like "holdfasts" to snails that rasp away on the tubular stalks (known as stipes).

The maritime fur trade resulted in the sea otter becoming extirpated (locally extinct) on Vancouver Island's west coast. A population was reintroduced in 1969 to 1972, and the mammals are now sometimes seen in the waters off Long Beach.

Now, where sea otters are recolonizing and expanding their range, the sea urchin population is being controlled once again. Shorelines not far from Long Beach that are strewn with cracked urchin, clam, and other shells indicate that the otters are eating their way back into the local scene and, in the process, helping restore the kelp habitat that has been largely absent for generations. Meanwhile, many residents trying to make a living harvesting the same shellfish the sea otters devour have a different view of this success story. They see the increased otter population as unfair competition threatening their livelihoods.

Will the ecological benefits of a rejuvenated kelp forest outweigh these concerns? The debate will continue. Nevertheless, in time, the view from Long Beach's interpretive centre may once again include an expanse of kelp forests, complete with the bobbing heads of otters visible among the glistening kelp fronds.

been virtually wiped out. The otter hunt business finally ground to a halt. It's estimated that before the era of the pelt trade, the population of sea otters on the Pacific coast between Japan and Baja California was about 300,000. Even by 1911, when legislation was first enacted to protect sea otters, fewer than 2,000 of the animals were thought to remain.

Island Settlement Spreads West

The years following the sea otter trade were ones of great transition, particularly for the First Nations. The Tla-o-qui-aht, Yuu-cluth-aht, and neighbouring nations were still living much as they had for generations, travelling throughout their territories as the seasons and resources dictated. However, their numbers were declining. The *mamalhni* ("those whose houses float on the water") may have left temporarily, but the intense period of trade had profoundly changed the reality for the indigenous residents. The introduction of firearms radically altered the dynamics of warfare, and the spreading of previously unknown illnesses such as smallpox eroded populations. Groups began to merge in response. Today's Yuu-cluth-aht First Nation, for example, is thought to be an amalgamation of seven distinct groups.

First Nations had their own systems of trade and commerce long before the *mamalhni* arrived, but the sea otter trade era had introduced a new model of commerce with access to novel goods and new sources of wealth. Chiefs began to factor in the harvest of resources for trade not only with other First Nations, but also with new foreign visitors to their territories. What no one had counted on was that the visitors would start unpacking their bags, intending to stay.

After years of jockeying with the Spanish and the Americans, the British finally gained control of the west coast. In 1843, the Hudson's Bay Company began building a trading post at the southern tip of Vancouver Island, having been granted a twenty-one-year exclusive trading and hunting licence in the northwest by the British Crown.

After building a fort out of the Douglas fir forest in what is now the city of Victoria, foreign presence on Vancouver Island grew. Island lands had been granted to the Hudson's Bay Company on condition that it would open up the region for settlement. With the signing of the Oregon Boundary Treaty on June 15, 1846, the border between the United States and British Canada was finally settled. For a decade or so, Victoria remained a small community of fewer than a thousand people, with activities centred on the Hudson's Bay Company post. Then, with the discovery of gold on the Fraser River in 1858, hundreds of people, the vast majority being single men, flooded into Fort Victoria. Although many passed through en route to seeking their fortunes, some stayed on, looking for opportunity on the island.

William Banfield was one of the first of these early settlers to be curious as to what lay north of Victoria. He arrived in 1848 at Esquimalt Harbour, near Victoria, on the British man-of-war HMS *Constance*, the first ship to christen the colony's naval port. After his discharge from the navy, Banfield switched to a sloop and ventured up the coast. As he travelled, he kept an eye open for opportunities for settlers. He was much impressed with the untapped potential he saw all around him.

In the summer of 1858, the *Daily Victoria Gazette* published eight front-page articles by Banfield in which he gave a first-hand account of an area that most people at the time imagined as being a forested void. Reporting on his travels between Sooke and Clayoquot Sound, he described the native people and their activities, possibilities for settlement, and the wealth of natural resources available: timber, salmon, seals, elk, bear, and whales.

On October 24, 1859, William Banfield wrote to the Colonial Secretary, "A chart, Sir, or tracing of a good chart, would be of infinite service." His request was answered in 1861 when the colonial government assigned George H. Richards, a British naval officer, to lead an extensive coastal survey. With the paddle-sloop *Hecate* serving as the mother ship and up to seven small boats working from her at a time, the convoluted and multi-featured coastline was painstakingly plotted. The result was the first detailed charts of the west coast of Vancouver Island, including the Long Beach area.

As part of their survey work, Richards and his assistant, Daniel Pender, were also responsible for assigning place names. Having scant knowledge of local history, they typically applied names that were a nod to fellow officers on their or other British ships—names with little connection to the area. Gowlland Rocks, for instance, was named for John Gowlland, the surveyor with Captain Richards's coastal survey.

Along with the charts, Richards and Pender compiled a two-volume *Vancouver Island Pilot*, for use by coastal mariners. It included instructions on how to approach the shoreline, observations about native people and other residents, and information on where supplies might be procured. Describing the island's west coast in general, Richards is frank. He wrote, "It is fringed by rocks and hidden dangers, especially near the entrances to the sounds, and the exercise of great caution and vigilance will be necessary..."

Although Banfield did not write specifically about Long Beach, he did give some idea of the native presence, describing the settlement of about 450 "Youcloulyets" in a harbour (Ucluelet Inlet) "facing to the south but not at all exposed to the Pacific Ocean—equally sheltered and five times as large as the estuary at Victoria." He was smitten with their home, writing that "nature in her most generous gifts, never formed a more splendid assemblage of harbors or inland waters, adapted for steam navigation in whose vicinity fine lumber land abounds." Clearly, people were reading Banfield's articles and listening to reports trickling into Victoria about the west coast. From the 1860s onward, enterprising men came searching for resources. Soon his reports mention American ships coming into Alberni to load wood spars or to trade potatoes and flour. The building of a few new trading posts and a second intense era of fur hunting and trading, this time in fur seal pelts, were some of the outcomes of this expanded exploration on the west coast.

A prevailing attitude of the era—that uncultivated land was not used or owned—certainly helped the colonial expansionist cause. In 1868, Gilbert Malcolm Sproat wrote of how he explained the forced acquisition of land at the end of Alberni Inlet for a sawmill to the Tseshaht people living there: "I sent a boat for the chief, and explained to him that his tribe must move their encampment, as we had bought all the surrounding land from the Queen of England, and wished to occupy the site of the village for a particular purpose. He replied that the land belonged to themselves, but that they were willing to sell it. The price not being excessive, I paid him what was asked—about twenty pounds' worth of goods—for the sake of peace, on condition that the whole people and buildings should be removed the next day."

The Soul Searchers

Wherever traders and explorers have pushed new pathways in the world, missionaries have followed. And so it happened on Vancouver Island's west coast. In the fall of 1874, Father Augustin J. Brabant travelled to the Long Beach area along with Bishop Charles J. Seghers in search of a location for a west coast mission. They chose Hesquiat at the northern end of Clayoquot Sound, but on this trip the two missionaries also became among the first (and possibly *the* first) non-native people to walk the shores of Long Beach.

They had travelled to the native village of Ittatsoo, in what is now Ucluelet Harbour, by sealing schooner and then up the outside coast by canoe. On their way home, they stopped in at the Tla-o-qui-aht village of Opitsat, requesting transportation to Ucluelet. The chief agreed, but first wanted to take them up to his fishing camp on the Kennedy River. From there, he would walk them over to Long Beach, where they would launch a canoe and paddle to Ucluelet.

Once they reached Long Beach, however, they found the seas too high to get through the breakers and were forced to stay put. For two days, Father Brabant and Bishop Seghers camped and waited there. What they thought of the stunning stretch of sand we will never know, for they make little mention of the site, merely writing that it was "a beautiful sandy beach."

Finally, when the sea conditions did not subside, the men decided to walk to Ucluelet. They had two guides from Kyuquot with them, but neither of those men was familiar with the area. Despite having received instructions on where to look for the trails connecting Florencia Bay to Ucluelet Harbour, the group got lost several times flailing about in the bush. Heavy rains ruined their campsites and a fire they made grew so large that it burned

THE WRECK OF THE *FLORENCIA*

The Peruvian brigantine Florencia left Utsalady, in Washington's Puget Sound, on November 8, 1860, carrying a load of lumber. Caught days later in a storm off Cape Flattery, she took on water and struggled to stay upright for more than two hours as her load shifted in the pummelling seas. Four men—the captain, cook, ship's owner, and a passenger from Victoria—disappeared overboard, leaving the second mate and four crewmen to fight on. The storm tore loose much of the ship's rigging and swept away the casks of fresh water.

For more than two weeks, the *Florencia* limped along with no help in sight. The crew were able to distill salt water for drinking but with every day became increasingly hungry and weak. They finally received food and fresh water from a passing ship near Nootka Sound, about 110 nautical miles northwest of Cape Flattery, but an attempt by the HMS *Forward* to tow the struggling ship failed.

Alone again, the brigantine drifted back south for eight days before finally managing to drop anchor in an open bay. The respite was brief. When the anchor began to drag, the exhausted crew prepared to abandon ship. They cobbled together a raft, loaded their stove, a topsail, and themselves aboard, and headed for land through the heaving seas. The raft capsized, and the men were tumbled into the waves. Fortunately, several native men pulled the severely weakened sailors out of the water. The rescuers then warmed and fed the wreck's survivors before taking them to Ucluelet.

The *Florencia* subsequently ground ashore and broke apart in the bay that today bears her name. Captain Richards officially bestowed the name during his 1861 survey, but for some, the official name never really stuck. Many local residents call it Wreck Bay.

their shoes and clothing. Then hunger set in. At one point, "the Bishop took a fainting fit," wrote Brabant. "He lay down on the rocks and asked if I had any food left. I took down the satchel which I had on my back and after careful examination I found a few grains of sugar and a little flour in the corner of an old flour sack. This I gathered in a spoon and presented to His Lordship."

When they eventually thought to pay attention to what their native companions were eating, they regained some strength dining on raw mussels and salal berries. Eventually they made it to their destination.

Brabant remained a presence on the coast for years, overseeing the Hesquiat mission and other enterprises of the church in the area. It's not clear if he ever returned to Long Beach, but he never wrote of it again.

4

the fortune seekers arrive

TRAVELLING WEST toward the coast on Highway 4, the road twice crosses Lost Shoe Creek as it nears the Ucluelet-Tofino T-junction. This creek starts in the hills north of Ucluelet and, thirteen winding kilometres (eight miles) later, empties into the ocean at Florencia Bay. Not surprisingly, you can often see a shoe or two propped up on one of the bridge railings, left by passersby—a gesture that might amuse W.E. Sutton, were he here today. The creek got its name in a very literal way when Sutton passed by in February 1903, en route to visit his brother's mining claim. Sutton fought valiantly to wrench his way through the wall of salal to get to the beach at Florencia Bay, finally deducing that it was more effective to roll over the barrier than struggle within it.

Successful as that technique might have been, he promptly lost a shoe while fording the creek that spilled out onto the beach. As he later stated matter-of-factly in a lecture in Victoria, "I named it Lost Shoe Creek because I lost my shoe there."

I think of Sutton whenever I visit this creek where it meets the Florencia Bay sands. I also wonder if he would recognize the place and the forest that surrounds it, for much has changed in the century since he waded here. Today, Lost Shoe Creek could be aptly named Lost Salmon Creek, as a walk along its lower section reveals.

In the late 1960s, when the federal and provincial governments were negotiating to have land put aside for a national park, Western Forest Products, which held tenure in much of the Crown forests at the time, began "highgrading" near the creek. They cut wide swathes of forest but removed only the most lucrative trees. The rest were left on the ground. Before the boundaries of the park reserve were finally agreed on in 1970, more than 26 percent of the land in what is now the Long Beach Unit of the reserve had been clear-cut in this way, including much of the land around Lost Shoe Creek.

The area was later replanted at one go, but the tree seedlings were never thinned. (Moreover, much of it was replanted with Douglas fir, a species that grows well on drier parts of the island but not on the wet west coast.) The result: a forest of even-aged, crowded, spindly trees. So dense is the growth that little light can reach the forest floor. Where a plush, three-dimensional understory would be found in a healthy rainforest, here is a comparative desert.

As if the cut-and-run madness wasn't injury enough, the removal of trees right up to the creek's banks in some sections both destroyed streamside (riparian) habitat and clogged the creek with post-pillage debris. In the coastal forest, riparian vegetation is critical to a healthy stream and its salmon runs. Conifers and shrubs such as salal and huckleberries shade streams, regulating their temperature for salmon and other species. The plants' roots stabilize stream banks, minimizing erosion and siltation. Their bark, leaves, needles, and berries rain into the streams, feeding insects, which in turn feed the salmon.

After the logging, Lost Shoe Creek, and Sandhill Creek up at Long Beach, were left an ecological mess.

Fortunately, there's now hope of righting the condition of the creek and its adjoining lands. Today, more than forty years since the damage was done, the Kennedy Watershed Restoration Project is making progress in restoring the hydrological, biological, and ecological integrity of Lost Shoe Creek and other watercourses in the area. By removing the choking debris and thinning stands so that sunlight can once again reach down to the photon-starved earth, crews are restoring the ecosystem to the way it was when W.E. Sutton tumbled over the salal and made his way down to the mouth of the creek.

This quick grab for trees before the land was locked up in a national park was an echo of an earlier time at Lost Shoe Creek, when men were also trying to make a buck from the region's resources.

Gold!

Klih-wi-tu-a was the first to find what so many men were scouring Vancouver Island's western shores for. It was the summer of 1899, and steamships chugging up and down the coast were a regular sight, smoke trailing from their stacks. The steamers ran a scheduled service out of Victoria, delivering passengers to an array of new settlements springing up: trading posts at Ucluelet

SALAL: CURSE OF THE COAST

W.E. Sutton's ordeal during his trek to Florencia Bay was par for the course for early travellers in the Long Beach area. Gaining access to the shoreline from land or to the land from the shore inevitably meant doing battle with that seemingly innocent brush foe: salal. This densely growing shrub of shiny, leathery evergreen leaves is found in most marine edges of the Pacific Northwest, but on outer coastal regions, it grows and spreads at its magnificent, robust best. Reaching heights of five metres (sixteen feet) and often tightly interwoven with its neighbours, it can form a glossy green, near-impenetrable wall.

George Smith, a timber surveyor in the area in the 1890s, described his feelings about the plant this way: "It was the toughest work I believe I ever had. It was almost continual sallal [sic] anywhere from six to ten feet high… The sallal nearly got us! When we boarded the steamer at Ucluelet, we were a tough looking outfit. A very nice old lady in Victoria asked me why so many young surveyors take to drink and I said I didn't know, but that there was a plant on the West Coast called sallal that might easily account in part for it."

Today, salal can still be a formidable obstacle for anyone hoping to bushwhack or clear a trail through the coastal forest. Once established, it grows fast, spreading vigorously via underground stems, so any previous hard work to eradicate it can be obliterated in short order. Nevertheless, its abundance and the fact that the shrub's branches and leaves hold their shape and freshness so well makes salal popular greenery for flower arrangements.

Two friends learned this in 1996 when they went for a walk at Long Beach and saw a large container from a commercial ship in the breakers near shore. They knew the container could be filled with all manner of goods that are shipped overseas—computers, televisions, sports equipment, and such. What bounty awaited them? Just as they arrived at the container, it bounced in the surf and hit the beach, and the doors flew open. Inside was revealed boxes of "florist-grade" salal destined for New Zealand, picked in Washington State.

and Clayoquot, a sawmill in Ucluelet Harbour, a Catholic mission at Hesquiat, scattered pre-emptions here and there, and hotels at Clayoquot and the head of the Bear (Bedwell) River.

The fur seal trade and missionary work brought many new-comers, but the big pull at the end of the nineteenth century was prospecting, with waves of men arriving to seek their fortune in the rocks of Vancouver Island. Almost any mineral in quantity piqued interest, but "Tyee Jack," the English name given to Klih-wi-tu-a, started the area's first major gold rush when he spotted sparkles in the sand at Florencia Bay.

Tyee Jack wasn't alone the day he discovered gold. He was helping Carl "Cap" Binns deliver the mail from Ucluelet to Clayo-quot. It's not clear whether Jack already knew there was gold to be found on the beach and just happened to spot some and point it out to Binns that day or whether this was indeed a discovery for both men.

Either way, the result was the same in a part of the world still in the grips of a forty-year bout of gold fever. Ever since gold had been discovered on the Fraser River in 1858 and soon after in the Cariboo, the west coast's main port, Victoria, had been inun-dated periodically with men arriving, outfitting themselves, and heading out to the gold fields. By the late 1890s, they were flood-ing into Victoria anew on their way to the latest El Dorado, the gold fields of the Yukon.

At the time of Jack's discovery near Long Beach, the area had few non-native settlers. The 1898 voters list for Ucluelet, for example, had only thirteen men on it: six farmers, two butchers, one carpenter, two lumbermen, one missionary, and one gar-dener. In no time, however, Jack and Binns's news had ignited a small boom.

Binns had arrived on the coast in 1895 with William Thompson after the pair sailed from Ireland on the *Lucipara*. They rowed into Ucluelet harbour, and family lore has it that Binns disembarked in a foxtail coat and silk shirt. If so, he was wildly overdressed for his wild new home. He and Thompson started a small trading post together and each established a homestead.

Discovering gold handed Binns a new profession. Along with Thompson and a few others, he quickly formed the Ucluelet Placer Mining Company, and the group hightailed it back out along the rough trail to Florencia Bay. (Apparently, Binns graciously included a portion in the claim for his co-discoverer, but subsequent mentions of Tyee Jack are few.) Officially first on the scene, they hammered a stake into the ground with a notice of intent to file a claim. Sorting out the paperwork in Victoria would come later.

Binns and his partners weren't alone on the beach for long. With the regular comings and goings of coastal steamers, glittering secrets were impossible to keep. In a matter of weeks, the Victoria *British Colonist* newspaper was shouting "Gold!" for all to hear. On July 13, 1899, it reported:

> While all the world has been looking to the Klondike, Cape Nome, Galovin Bay and other equally remote and inhospitable corners of the globe for gold, the precious District has, it is said, been waiting to be won at a point on the West Coast of this island, not 100 miles from Victoria by direct line and if reports be true, in quantity sufficient to bring 10,000 miners to the field in half a year.

Early news reports from mining efforts were promising. Mr. McKenzie, a storekeeper from Dodger's Cove in Barkley Sound, "cleaned up" $9 in a single day "with the crudest possible

Carl Binns and James Sutton were two of the first Wreck Bay gold miners. Like other early miners of the area, they used simple tools initially, including gold pans and rockers, to separate the gold from the sand.

appliances." And Joe Drinkwater, who had been sniffing around for gold up in Clayoquot Sound, "took up a pan of sand haphazard and washed it in the presence of an interested group, the return being $2.40."

Claims were quickly made and partnerships forged overnight. Captain Hackett, of the fur sealing schooner *Libbie,* heard of the find while he was in the area looking to sign on a native crew for the upcoming season. Putting that search on the back burner, he headed down to Wreck Bay and there paid $50 for interest in a claim that had been staked only the day before. Soon after, Captain Victor Jacobson of the sealing schooner *Minnie* and Reverend Swartout of Ucluelet both invested in Hackett's portion of the claim. And so it went.

That the gold occurred not as nuggets but more like pow-
der introduced a wrinkle the area's first miners hadn't counted
on. Trying to separate the gold from the sand was frustratingly
hard work, like trying to sift pepper from flour. Still, this wasn't
enough to deflate big dreams, and for several months, enthusiasm over the possibilities for Florencia Bay's lode continued
to bubble. Almost daily, the *British Colonist* reported who was
coming and going from the site. Tantalizing bits of information, such as the arrival in Victoria of "San Francisco capitalists"
and "black sand experts" kept spirits buoyed. So did the steady
reports on the value of the gold sent out from Florencia Bay in
steamship vaults: $1,000 on July 14; $900 on July 18; $1,265
on August 12; $1,400 on August 19... Hopes also ran high that
new techno-wizardry such as tubular amalgamators and "copper plate gold-savers"—machines that used electrolysis to
capture the gold on metal plates—would soon see a serious boost
to yields.

LOADS OF LUMBER FOR PANS OF GOLD

> When a man finds value in a rock it affects his thinking. He
> may have seen only two dollars' worth of gold but he'll run
> around looking for twenty thousand to develop it.
> > *–from the novel* Florencia Bay, *by James McNamee.*

Despite reports of some people "cleaning up," the majority
of men working in the area were getting little return for their
effort. Part of the difficulty was the lack of fresh water needed
for the pans and sluices. Seawater wouldn't work—it was full
of sand and difficult to harness from the waves crashing onto
the beach. In the summer of 1900, a group of miners banded

The Wreck Bay flume was an ambitious and expensive attempt to tease gold from the sand at Florencia Bay. At one point, twenty-five men were constructing the flume while another fifteen worked the sluices.

together and came up with an ambitious plan. Pooling their resources, they proceeded to build a wooden flume almost a mile long, supported on a wooden trestle, to capture the flow of fresh water coursing down Lost Shoe Creek and carry the water along the length of the beach.

It was a significant project, reportedly costing $10,000, an enormous sum for the time. About 14,000 metres (45,000 feet) of lumber went into the posts and crossbars of the trestle and the long chute-like flume it supported, raised at some points as high as 4.5 metres (15 feet) above the beach. Two bridges also had to be constructed across Lost Shoe Creek: one 24 metres (79 feet) long and the other 46 metres (151 feet) long.

Building the flume structure took ingenuity. Unloading the delivered lumber from steamships offshore at Wreck Bay took nerve.

The miners had to row out to meet the ships. If the seas co-operated, the ship anchored in the entrance to the bay, staying well outside the zone of breaking waves. The miners then manoeuvred their rowboats alongside and scrambled aboard to help bundle and lower the lumber into the water, where they were towed in toward shore. The harder task was to get back through the breakers and onto land without letting the surf turn the lumber bundles into torpedoes that could flip or damage a boat and, worse, injure a man.

In the end, however, the grand installation was no match for the west coast's conditions. The first blow came in late October, when storm seas and high tides tore away part of the flume. As winter set in, miner after miner retreated, frustrated by the wind and sea undoing a year's work. The *Colonist* resumed with enthusiastic missives during the summer of 1901, but the possibility of a big strike at Florencia Bay never again reached the heights it had in 1900. Some men persisted for a few more years, working their claims using less grandiose methods than the flume—they were back to pans and sluice boxes—but most were eventually worn down by the west coast's weather.

GOLD FEVER LEGACY: MORE SPECULATORS THAN SPECKS
Although the chapter of earnest mining at Florencia Bay was lean and short-lived, its greater, longer-lasting yield was the influx of new settlers. The 1901 census for Ucluelet lists 105 residents, including women and children. Less than 2 years after the discovery at Florencia Bay, a third of that population was involved in gold mining.

Long after gold fever waned, Wreck Bay remained a popular day trip for the residents of Ucluelet, as shown in this photograph of a community picnic, circa 1912.

In all, about $40,000 worth of gold came off Florencia Bay in those first few years. However, a few ever-hopeful men continued to work their claims with pans and sluice boxes for years afterward, never quite able to release the dream. Alfred Carmichael, a former placer miner in the Atlin goldfields from 1899 to 1907, arrived on the west coast in the 1930s to investigate firsthand the scene at Wreck Bay. He sampled the sand and clay and had them analyzed at the provincial assay office. His samples revealed only a trace of gold.

Carmichael kept a journal of his trip and later wrote short essays about his stay and the wishful miners he met there. "Found one," he wrote, "an old Klondyk [sic] miner who lost his legs overseas, burning off the beach logs to get at the... sands.

In the 1930s, ever-hopeful miner Andrew Murison built a comfortable three-room home at Wreck Bay and kept a well-established garden of carrots, turnips, potatoes, lettuce, cabbage, and mint. He diverted a small stream through a wooden culvert to flow across the front of his property.

Later he told me that they found that there was gold caught in the rough wave worn skin of the logs and by burning them and sluicing out the ashes they got the gold."

Carmichael also visited Andrew Murison, a Scotsman who had been working the beach for five years or so. On the back page of his journal, Carmichael noted that "Mr. Murison was one of the many in the mad rush to the Nome gold fields in 1900 and was one of the fortunate ones, but like many more of the real pioneers and prospectors who have the qualities to 'go get it' but not the capacity to keep it. And having mismanaged the first million, he went after another one, and is still at it."

Murison worked three sluice boxes, and Carmichael noted that he "found success in short shifts of work, eating when he felt like it. He always lay down after eating and had a pipe." Murison also filled some of his days writing poetry, including this tribute to his home:

> I love it! I love it and who will say nay,
> To the beauty and charm of lovely Wreck Bay.
> The sunsets are 'luring, the breakers enduring.
> In calm and in storm it always has the form
> Of a Power that is greater than man can see,
> Which will ever remain a mystery.
> The horse shoe curve sweeps round so grand
> With Florencia Isle in the break of the band.
> Its setting is perfect. Oh who can gainsay,
> The beauty and charm of lovely Wreck Bay!

Shipwrecks and Rescuers

> The body of a well-dressed man was picked up on Long Beach near Schooner Cove, Clayoquot, by George Gray, an Indian. Papers were found in the pockets with the name George Woolridge, also a bible . . . , a book of blank bank checks, silver watch, Canadian Pacific Railway ticket and $60 in cash. The body is in very bad shape and held together mainly by clothing.
> *—February 9, 1906, the* British Colonist

From the late 1800s, the increased interest in the west coast for missionaries, traders, miners, settlers, and entrepreneurs led to an increase in ship's traffic—from small sloops to multisailed barquentines to steamships. It also led to an increase in shipwrecks.

In peril, the Chilean barque *Carelmapu* hoisted flags signalling distress into the rigging. Shortly after leaving Tofino, the ship was noticed by Captain Gillam of the CPR passenger steamship *Princess Maquinna,* who made several attempts to assist the vessel.

For dozens, perhaps hundreds, of shipwrecked mariners and passengers, the treacherous west coast of Vancouver Island, including Long Beach, became their last resting place. The bodies of some were found and identified, but most disappeared into the watery depths, taking their names and stories with them. Woolridge was a victim of the wreck of the *Valencia,* which took two agonizing days to break up off Pachena Point, south of Bamfield, after wrecking there January 21, 1906, leaving at least 117 people dead. Many bodies were never recovered. In that respect at least, Woolridge was one of the lucky ones.

Vancouver Island's west coast is often referred to as the Graveyard of the Pacific. Dozens of shipwrecks are known about, but many others went unrecorded. Several of the known wrecks came to rest on or near Long Beach. Most notable of these are the *Mustang* (1866), the *General Cobb* (1880), the *Carelmapu* (1915), and a mysterious Spanish "ghost ship" that apparently appeared and disappeared for years in the shifting sands between Green Point and Incinerator.

Common to many of the stories of the plight of these ships were the efforts of the area's residents, native and settler, who time and again went to heroic lengths in their efforts to rescue shipwrecked sailors. Search parties went looking for survivors and gave them shelter, water, and food. Bodies found were buried. This was the case with the *Carelmapu*, a three-masted Chilean barque that ran into trouble near the entrance to Juan de Fuca Strait on November 23, 1915. A storm blew the ship off-course up the coast, shredding its sails in the process. For two days, the lame ship drifted as the storm continued to push it perilously close to Vancouver Island's rocky outer shores. On November 25, now close to Long Beach, the crew had no choice but to drop anchor in the pounding open seas to try to keep the vessel from being heaved ashore.

Despite the wild sea conditions and having a complement of passengers, the CPR steamship *Princess Maquinna* made a valiant attempt to save the barque's crew, but it was forced to give up and leave when it, too, came in danger of wrecking. Those on the *Maquinna* could only watch as life boats lowered from the *Carelmapu* quickly flipped in the heaving waters, tossing the occupants into the sea and to certain death.

Eventually, the battered *Carelmapu* ground ashore near Gowlland Rocks, up the coast from Schooner Cove at the north end of Long Beach. As it listed, more crew members were washed overboard and lost. Only four men, the cabin boy, and the ship's dog (a Great Dane) miraculously managed to swim through the

THE RAINFOREST'S GIANTS

In the open spray zone close to the ocean's edge, Sitka spruce thrives in the constant saltwater misting, growing into thick, stunted, wind-sheered wedges that collectively create a spruce fringe. Along with natural barricades of salal, these walls of Sitka spruce must have made any shipwreck survivor staggering ashore think this was deliverance to just another version of Hell.

Yet, tuck in behind the spruce fringe on a windy day and you'll find a place of relative calm. The corps of volunteers dug in along this front line in the spruce fringe windbreak is what enables the forest behind to get on with the job of growing upright, very tall, and very old. Here, the sheltered Sitka spruce excels, with some specimens counting among the largest trees in the world. On nearby Meares Island, just off Tofino, stands a Sitka spruce that measures 13.7 metres (44.9 feet) around at its base and 48.8 metres (160.1 feet) from the ground to its broken top—about the height of a 10-storey building. The world's tallest Sitka spruce, at 96 metres (315 feet), is just down the coast from Long Beach at Carmanah Creek, on the boundary of the West Coast Trail section of Pacific Rim National Park. Many of these giants are more than 800 years old.

While Sitka spruce may win in the coastal rainforest's height category, western hemlock receives the award for greatest number. It is the most common tree species here, distinguishable by its short, flat, densely packed needles and the permanent droop to its tip. Meanwhile, western redcedar, the tree most closely woven into the fabric of Nuu-chah-nulth culture, completes the triumvirate of coastal rainforest conifers.

Shade for all of these conifers is not a problem. Their small but abundant needles provide hectares of photon-capturing surface area per tree so that whatever light filters through the dense forest canopy

In a west coast rainforest, the tips of the giant trees, mostly western hemlock, western redcedar, and Sitka spruce, comb the air around them for moisture. Fog and mist condense on the needles and drip to the forest floor.

can be gleaned. And, unlike the long taproot of other trees, the roots of these species spread horizontally, searching for and taking in nutrients in the shallow, acidic, nutrient-leached soils.

While the coastal rainforest's huge conifers garner most of the ecosystem's glory, they owe much of their health and survival to a complex support network of smaller plant species of varying ages and sizes. Even dead trees, standing or fallen, provide critical habitat for new growth. Nearly 97 percent of western hemlocks, for instance, get their start as seedlings on a fallen log.

heaving seas to the beach. (One of the men was a Hawaiian sea-man, Antonio Okione. According to local lore, he surfed ashore using a plank from the wreck.) The survivors took shelter in a shack there and were rescued by three Tofino men who had hiked through the night to the get to the wreck site. Over the next few days, the remains of several of the *Carelmapu*'s crew washed ashore, usually terribly battered by the sea and, more often than not, headless. Local residents helped in searching for them and in burying them on the shores of Long Beach.

In the wreck of the *Carelmapu* and in countless other wrecks, native people along Vancouver Island's west coast proved invalu-able. They relayed word of the location of wrecks, helped recover and bury bodies, and conducted rescues themselves. The sig-nificant efforts of the native people in helping survivors of the wrecked *General Cobb* in January 1880 received particular recog-nition. The American barque ran aground near Portland Point at the northwest end of Long Beach. Several Tla-o-qui-aht men res-cued the ship's crew by canoe and delivered them to Clayoquot. There, the survivors rested for a few days before being paddled to Barkley Sound by their Tla-o-qui-aht rescuers where they boarded the schooner *Alert* for Victoria. Six months later, the U.S. consul travelled to Clayoquot to personally thank the Tla-o-qui-aht people for their bravery and generosity and to present them with a large quantity of rice, "hard bread," molasses, and sugar.

The expression of gratitude didn't stop there. Almost a year later, a large contingent of Tla-o-qui-aht people gathered in Vic-toria to watch the U.S. consul present a medal to "Schewish, chief of the Clayoquots" in honour of their efforts to "save, kindly treat and care for the poor wrecked seaman." Gold medals or not, native people continued to assist those who needed help, on the Long Beach shores and elsewhere along the west coast.

5

fields of dreams and dreamers

T'S THE day after Christmas and my husband, daughters, and I have dragged our stuffed bodies off our respective couches and headed out for fresh air. We've driven from our home in Tofino and launched our inflatable boat at Grice Bay to cruise the shallow waters over the mudflats. This was once called Mud Bay for good reason.

Our cherry-red boat and orange floatation vests are the bright spots of colour in the muted winter landscape. The afternoon's water is dark and calm, soft rain pinging its surface gently. The sky is overcast, one cloud with no beginning or end, like a ceiling swathed in dove-grey velvet. In this light, the forests rimming the bay look like flat, slate-coloured brushstrokes rendered by an abstract painter to evoke a dark, wet background.

71

The outboard engine purrs in the quiet as we motor on a route that was used by west coast people for millennia. Long before motorized boats were even dreamt of, people paddled into the inlet, usually on the flooding tide, letting the ocean do much of the manual labour, propelling them up the bay and delivering them at high tide within easy access of the footpath and the short hike across the peninsula to Long Beach. The Tla-o-qui-aht people call this route *t'ashii,* the trail. First Nations and others have long harvested and hunted at these and other area mudflats.

Through binoculars, we watch the waterfowl drifting about unbothered by our presence. It's a haven here for dozens of overwintering species—grebe, bufflehead, goldeneye, wigeon, pintails, and scaups. Near the head of the bay, several white silhouettes stand out against the dark backdrop of the forest: six swans a-swimming, seemingly in honour of the yuletide season. A little deeper into the bay, we cut the engine and spend a moment doing our best wolf howls and then listening intently for a response. Silence is our only answer that day, but it doesn't mean we're not being observed. Wolves often travel the shoreline here, using it as a corridor between parts of their habitat as well as a hunting ground. This winter, Canada geese have been plentiful on the *Canis lupus* menu.

The tide has been turning, and the mudflats slowly start emerging as the water ebbs. It's time for us to leave while there's still enough water. At low tide, the little bay we've ducked into becomes a field of sorts, a slough of salt-tolerant plants, such as sea asparagus, salt grasses, silverweed, and Lyngby's sedge. "Field" is a loose term for these flats, as they are nothing like the grassy meadows or open range that cattle need. And they are a walker's minefield of boggy hummocks, ready to give way under the slightest weight, and ankle-snapping holes. At the edge of the flats, where mud meets meadow, straggles a row of greying, off-kilter fence posts, no doubt set into place firm and upright decades ago. Like soldiers who haven't heard the war is over, they remain faithful to their positions as best they can though relief refuses to come.

It's not certain to whose hands these relics could trace their origin, but I wonder if they might have been Paul J. Wollan's. He pre-empted this lot in July 1896, which makes him one of the first of the early settlers to take a chance on building a life on the west coast. Whether Wollan's posts or those of another settler who came after him, these well-aged stakes—probably once vital parts in a robust fencing system to contain wayward cattle—today perform a more genteel purpose: supporting thick mats of frilly lichen and moss.

A Dollar an Acre

Flying over the Long Beach area, you can spot the lands that were worked hard by settlers like Paul J. Wollan. Red alders are a good indicator. These ecological pioneers point the way to where human pioneers tried to create a home on the west coast. The sun-loving, fast-growing deciduous trees are the first to sprout on cleared land. Wherever the forest has been opened up for a highway, trail, house site, or garden, alders seem to rush in like Nature's self-assigned medics. They are the vegetative vanguard that prepares the soil to receive the slow-growing, longer-lived conifers. A filamentous bacteria living on alder roots removes nitrogen, a necessary nutrient for most plants, from the air, "fixing" it in a form that is usable to successor plants.

The earliest records of settlers at Long Beach come from 1890, when James Goldstraw pre-empted a 50-hectare (120-acre) parcel at Schooner Cove. By 1893, he had at least 2 neighbours,

BIRDER'S PARADISE: THE GRICE BAY MUDFLATS

Prime real estate around these parts is clearly in the eye of the beholder. If you're drawn here for the sand, surf, and sunsets, the ocean side of Long Beach commands the biggest interest. But if you're attracted by the muck and sea-grass banquets, as tens of thousands of birds are annually, then it is the mudflats of Grice Bay and other nearby expanses of mud that would command top dollar.

That these mudflats can support flocks with hundreds, even thousands of birds, attests to their richness. Mud shrimp, clams, and worms burrow just below the surface. As the tide rises over the flats, slim blades of eelgrass rise up with it, and crabs and dozens of species of small fish move in. The flats of Grice Bay, within the national park boundary, and the extensive Arakun and Ducking flats nearer to Tofino, all become smorgasbords for avians during the annual spring shorebird migration.

The journey these birds undertake is nothing short of remarkable. The western sandpipers, for instance, might have set off from their wintering grounds in Panama and are on their way to Alaska, a distance of about eleven thousand kilometres (seven thousand miles). Along the way, they're joined by other migrating shorebirds, such as dunlins, dowitchers, whimbrels, and yellowlegs. Some of these birds weigh little more than a small granola bar. On their way north, they stop to refuel at regular intervals—San Francisco and Humboldt Bays in California, Grays Harbour in Washington, the Fraser River delta, and here, too—for just a day or two before carrying on to the Copper River delta in Alaska. There, eight million birds gather for one last group dinner, before dispersing to their northern breeding grounds for the summer.

Shorebirds are often called wind birds, an apt name for a bird that can be whisked along by prevailing winds at speeds of ninety to one hundred kilometres (fifty-six to sixty-two miles) per hour. Their own flapping may gain the birds speeds of forty kilometres (twenty-five miles) per hour or so; the rest of the work is done by the wind. All that

Flocks of shorebirds move with such precision and in unison that they could make a choreographer weep. Each spring, west coast communities celebrate the flocks' return with a shorebird festival. Although the birds linger only a few days, the mudflats and beaches are important rest and feeding stops for them.

flying time burns up enormous amounts of energy, so at spots like the local mudflats, the birds feast, probing the sand and muck for molluscs, amphipods, worms, and other invertebrates. Some will even slurp up the biofilm—the brownish-green growth of diatoms on the mud's surface. Depending on the weather, they may stay for a couple of days of feeding, moving between the mudflats and the sands of Long Beach and Chesterman Beach near Tofino, taking advantage of the bounty reliably delivered during every shift of the tide.

William Kershaw and George Maltby. On a coast so sparsely populated, having and being a good neighbour could make all the difference.

All three men began to clear land and build small structures. They were joined at the cove by surveyor J.A. Mahood on New Year's Eve 1893, who made his first survey notation on December 31. Perhaps the group raised a glass together that evening on the shores of Long Beach, toasting to a successful year in their new homes.

Keen to see Vancouver Island settled, the colonial government granted pre-emptions for next to nothing, with the agreement that if the land was "improved," it could be purchased after completion of a survey and verification of residency. "Improved" was code for cleared and perhaps ditched or fenced in preparation for farming or ranching. Goldstraw's and Kershaw's pre-emptions were on property known locally as the Burnt Lands because it had been opened by fire, a fact the men might not have known in the lands office, but which likely was a bonus when it came to clearing their respective properties. Maltby's 62-hectare (154-acre) lot, however, was heavily treed, though he, too, eventually managed to clear a sizeable space for a homestead.

Land records show that Goldstraw made only one payment of $40 three years after pre-empting. By 1909, his lot had changed hands, and he seemed to disappear from Long Beach. Kershaw and Maltby, in contrast, stuck it out, receiving the Crown grants for their land a few years after making improvements. Both men paid a dollar an acre for their land.

In these early days of settlement, men came and went like shorebirds in the spring. The promise of land was an enticing prospect, but the long, hard work of clearing it, with only hand tools and maybe an ox, could sink even the most buoyant of dreams. Land registers for the area show pre-emption after pre-emption with CANCELLED, REVERTED, or ABANDONED written next to the record. Sometimes the would-be farmers or ranchers left their land for a short time to make money elsewhere. Kershaw was one of those, moving back and forth between Victoria and his pre-emption for about ten years before he, like Goldstraw, left Long Beach for good.

Maltby was an exception, becoming a fixture on the west coast for the rest of his life. He, like all settlers, had to be resourceful and willing and able to serve as carpenter, farmer, hunter, cook, vet, and even doctor when the need arose. He once tended his badly cut foot by sticking it in a sack of flour. For days, he hobbled about his homestead with a bulky flour poultice swaddling his festering foot.

Although the land took most of his time, Maltby also picked up whatever work was available for wages. Carrying out the 1901 census was one of those jobs. Over three months the thirty-three-year-old rowed or sailed the length of his district from Long Beach up to Nootka Sound, stopping in at every homestead, trading post, mining camp, and tiny settlement along the way. Maltby also helped build sawmills in Ucluelet and at Mosquito Harbour on Meares Island, served as "road boss" on a crew building the first Tofino-to-Long Beach road, and acted as Justice of the Peace for a time.

George Maltby left Schooner Cove in 1911, moving to a lot closer to the growing communities of Tofino and Clayoquot. There, he started up a market garden and was long remembered as a cheerful soul, singing as he rowed his red dory down the inlet on the ebbing tide to deliver baskets of fresh produce.

Most of the earliest settlers were bachelors, but not all. In 1894, Jacob Arnet pre-empted 53 hectares (132 acres) on the protected waters of Mud Bay (now Grice Bay) across the peninsula from Maltby. Arnet had left his home in Trondhjem, Norway, in 1888 when he was 18. After a time working in Iowa, he migrated north to Canada, where he fished the Fraser River before being drawn to the large properties available for pre-emption on the west coast of Vancouver Island.

Arnet's land at the edge of a small creek afforded him a stunning view of Clayoquot Sound. A narrow channel winding through the mudflats permitted passage for a small rowboat or canoe on all but the lowest tides. It was a site ripe for sharing, as Arnet was soon to do.

On May 20, 1896, he travelled to Victoria, where, a week later, he married Johanna Johnsen, who had come from Norway with Arnet's brother August. Jacob and Johanna combined forces to work their west coast land, and near the end of 1897, their first child, daughter Alma, was born. By then, the homestead included a house, a barn, a large garden, and some fruit trees. The family also had cattle, which they let graze wild, periodically rounding one up for butchering. In time, the family grew, adding six sons.

Eventually, four of Jacob's brothers joined him on the coast, where the five became well known for their fishing skills. At first, they salted what they caught to preserve it, making their own barrels for storage, but later, the family became partners in the Clayoquot Sound Canning Company, near the mouth of the Kennedy River. Jacob built a small floathouse and in the summertime towed it to the cannery, with the children locked safely inside during the journey. While their parents worked, the Arnet siblings played on the shore with the native children whose parents helped in the cannery.

Although they were isolated, the Arnets were not the only family at Mud Bay. August Arnet built a home not far from Jacob and Johanna, and another Norwegian family, the Wingens, had a homestead and water-powered sawmill farther up the bay. With the requisite ingenuity of a successful pioneer, Thomas Wingen used huge beach stones as bearings for the nine-metre- (thirty-foot-) diameter waterwheel and yew and crabapple wood for the cogs. He kept the machinery lubricated with the oil of dogfish, a small shark. When he completed an order, he would raft up the lumber, put his small rowboat on *top* of the raft, then hoist a sail and deliver the shipment. The Wingen mill, as well as the Sutton brothers' mill in Ucluelet, provided lumber to many of the early settlers on the coast.

It is unclear how long the Arnets spent at Mud Bay, but by 1912, Jacob had moved his family to Tofino, where they built one of the first homes overlooking the inlet. Together, the five Arnet brothers and their large families accounted for a significant percentage of the town's population in the early days.

Long after they'd left the homestead, Jacob still travelled up through Mud Bay to Long Beach to hunt his cattle, which were by then feral in the forest.

The Long Beach Ranchers

On December 5, 1908, Frederick Gerald Tibbs penned a quick note to Walter Dawley, storekeeper at Clayoquot. "Please send 1 Box Pophams Pilot bread biscuits," he wrote in his flamboyant calligraphic hand. Tibbs wrote from his "Tidal Wave Ranch," perched on the cliff above Green Point at Long Bay, as Long Beach was then called. He was only twenty-two years old when he pre-empted Lot 141 in the fall of 1908. Fred Tibbs would have had a few neighbours at the time (George Maltby for one), but really the young British immigrant was quite isolated, apparently happily so, and set on his dream of carving a ranch out of

Fred Tibbs and his cousin, Vera Marshall. Tibbs was one of the earliest, and certainly one of the most colourful, settlers at Long Beach. His homestead was located in what today is Green Point Campground.

the wilderness. That he was not a rough-and-ready frontiersman was clear from early on. No doubt, he raised a few eyebrows at Clayoquot: for example, the time he sent a letter requesting "1 (20¢) tin of pink paint as nearly as possible as per pattern colour & oblige also 1 Gal. red roofing paint." Stapled to the note was a strip of pink ribbon and a swatch of wallpaper with pink roses.

Many early Long Beach settlers had a few cows, and perhaps an ox or a horse. But some, such as Charles Tupper Harvey, had a working farm and ranch. Harvey's ranch included Lot 162, land that today includes the Long Beach parking lots.

Why Tibbs made his way to the west coast will never be entirely clear. He was a good-natured Englishman from a family of considerable means. His niece and others speculated that a facial disfigurement, the result of a childhood accident, may have so embarrassed him that he wanted to move somewhere he wasn't known. Others said he was a remittance man, sent away from England by his family and given a regular allowance to get established well out of their hair. Neither reason quite fits Tibbs's apparent character and behaviour. For one, while Tibbs could be shy, particularly with women, he was affable, charming, and keen to participate in many facets presented by his new life on the coast, from political (he was active in the Clayoquot Conservative Association) to poetical (he was known to post a poem or two on the notice board at the Clayoquot store). For another, Tibbs displayed none of the scoundrel-type traits commonly associated with remittance men—too often chronic drinkers, gamblers, and philanderers. Rather, he seemed more refined in his tastes and expressiveness than many local settlers. The effusive letters he wrote to shopkeepers and the others stood well apart from the average missives they received. In one, for example, Tibbs concludes with the baffling, "Wishing you a New Year bringing you an early duplication and an improvement in the inclement inclinations of the denizens of the atmosphere."

Tibbs did get on with clearing a patch of land on the bluff and constructing a small log cabin. He had a stunning view of the ocean and the sands of Long Beach, curving out to either side. In the end, however, he didn't stay on the property long enough to see it become the ranch he'd envisioned. He came and went for a couple of years, spending part of the time away helping to construct a lighthouse on Triangle Island, an isolated rock about 300 kilometres (185 miles) northwest of Long Beach. But in 1912 or 1913, he decided to sell his property at Long Bay and buy a small island near the growing community of Tofino. He clearcut the island of all but one tall tree, around which he then built scaffolding and topped with a small platform. On occasion, he would climb up to the platform to play his cornet, or he would haul up his gramophone and serenade his neighbours with the latest musical recordings. He also built a wooden "castle," complete with tower, and painted the structure white with red and blue trim.

While Fred Tibbs may have planned to run cattle at Tidal Wave Ranch, it seems he never had any permanent company, four-legged or otherwise, on his bluff-with-a-view. Charles Tupper Harvey, though, had the real deal: a working ranch on

Another early Long Beach settler, William Sanford, homesteaded near Sand-hill Creek. He travelled the coast on foot with an ox and cart to help haul his supplies, stopping regularly at Ucluelet to sell butter from his cows.

the shores of Long Beach. On November 1, 1900, Harvey leased Sea View Farm on Long Bay from Clayoquot shopkeepers Thomas Stockham and Walter Dawley. The place came with eight cows, three steers, five heifers, a bull, a horse, and a mule and, as the agreement read, it was "to be occupied as a farm and cattle ranch."

All told, Harvey's ranch covered 129 hectares (319 acres), none of which was very suitable range. It reached over to Mud Bay and included about a mile of beachfront on Long Beach. The cattle roamed throughout the forested acreage and even onto the beach. Harvey did supply some feed for them, often ordering "chop" (ground grain) from Dawley's store, but mostly the cattle foraged for themselves.

Harvey took to the west coast ranging life. Within ten years after starting at Sea View Farm, he pre-empted and then purchased seven more lots in his own name, adding to his spread. An article in the *Victoria Daily Colonist* in 1913 reporting on the activities on the west coast remarks on Harvey's ranch, saying "[it] is notable in that its owner has 50 [head] of steer, which he manages to find pasture in the range about him and in a fine salt-water slough of 150 ac."

Linking Long Beach to the World

Letters sent by post, notes hand-delivered and, of course, messages passed by word of mouth were the main communication methods up and down the coast until the turn of the nineteenth century. Then, telegraph systems were established. Single strands of wire strung between trees and posts all along shorelines and rough trails connected coastal lighthouses, stores, canneries, mining camps, and other operations to each other and to the outside world. By 1902, most of the line in the Long Beach area was constructed and operational.

Men were hired to "walk the line" to check that the lines and poles were in good condition and that the trails these lines followed were clear and their bridges sound. As proper roads were built, the routes of the telegraph lines were shifted to run along the new roadsides. Not that road building happened with any haste, despite decades of effort by Long Beach–area residents in the form of stacks of pleading letters to politicians and newspapers, presentations packed with persuasive arguments, and meticulously laid-out plans.

With such a small and scattered population, the west coast was low on the priority list when the rest of the island, which

Linemen regularly walked their territories, stringing the wire lines and fixing any broken connections, which were numerous after storms. The line between Ucluelet and Tofino alternated between the rugged trail and muddy road and the forest at the edge of Long Beach.

was filling rapidly with immigrants, was in need of surveyors to lay out town sites and routes for road and rail. In a 1912 report, surveyor Alistair I. Robertson describes a road running from the end of Ucluelet Arm and then parallel to Florencia Bay and Long Beach through the forest. He reported "over three miles have been cleared and graded, and wagons have been taken as far as Lost Shoe Creek, over which a bridge was constructed this summer." Other road crews were at work in the area at the time, trying to link up Tofino and Ucluelet over the miles of forest still separating them, but progress remained frustratingly slow, and would stay that way for many more years.

Land for Profit

An 1899 advertorial in the *Victoria Daily Colonist* pulled out all the stops in trumpeting Vancouver Island's assets, from its "surfeit of magnificent scenery," "exceeding plenteousness," and wildlife riches (including herds of deer "disporting themselves on beaches") to the resort-worthy charms of Long Beach which, if it were on the American side of the border the article noted, "would long ere have been teeming with summer loungers, gay hotels and enthusiastic surf bathers."

This sort of hyperbole was not uncommon in an era where it was important to get settlers out onto the land. Promises of roads and railways were cast freely, as were tantalizing half-truths about the ease with which the bounty of the land and sea could be had by anyone with enterprise. Who wrote this article is unclear, but any number of businesses, governments, and local organizations of the day could have. Promoting the wonders of the land to prospective investors, settlers, and tourists brought out a surfeit of magnificent superlatives in all of them.

The Vancouver Island Development League was especially active on the west coast, sending members to Victoria to make presentations and also inviting delegates to be toured around. The group promoted the region's tourism potential, as well as its timber, fish, cheap land, and other resources. They weren't above using a prop or two, once bringing a slab of tree trunk, nearly 3.5 metres (11.5 feet) in diameter, to an event in Victoria.

Such zealous, proactive efforts led not only to settlement but soon to land speculation as well. In June 1909, for example, Fred Tibbs received a letter from the Island Investment Company, which began, "About the property you have for sale: we can sell it." Whether Tibbs took this organization up on its offer isn't clear, but within a few years, he had managed to sell his Long Beach property for about $5,000, a large sum for the time. Tibbs wasn't the only one being offered that kind of money and more. Another property on Long Beach, for example, bought by an M.P. Gordon for $1,000 on June 4, 1912, was sold five or six months later for $10,400.

With prices like these, lots were being purchased in no time as investments, sight unseen, and many by the unlikeliest of possible west coast settlers. The land records for Lots 134, 136, and 137 on Long Beach, between Green Point and Sandhill Creek, are an interesting case in point. All were purchased on September 16, 1908, each with a woman's name on the title: Ada Leverson, Violet Leverson, and Ruth Leverson. The common connection was Ernest Leverson, the son of a British diamond and pearl trader who had amassed a considerable fortune. Ernest worked in the trade as well, during which time he also briefly courted and then married nineteen-year-old Ada Beddington, twelve years his junior. They had a daughter, Violet, but the marriage was not a happy one. Ernest was not only a compulsive gambler with a bad temper, it turned out he was a liar, too. A little girl he had told Ada was his ward, and who was being raised in a Paris convent, was in fact his first daughter, Ruth.

When Ernest lost the family's money in a bad investment, he and Ada separated for good. Ernest's father agreed to settle his son's debts and to give him a fresh start in the lumber business in Canada, where, as Violet later wrote, "it was hoped he would

THE WILD DOGS AND CATS OF LONG BEACH

Remarkably, in all the accounts of life at Long Beach in the late 1800s and early 1900s, wolves and cougars are rarely mentioned. This record (or lack of it) is telling in how much attitudes about wilderness predators have changed. The view in the early settlement days of the west coast was no different than that in most other places in North America. Wild mammals, especially big ones, were seen as threats to livestock and to people and were, for the most part, vilified. A "wolf and panther destruction bill" passed by the colonial government of British Columbia in 1869 put both species in settlers' gun sights.

For the first half of the 1900s, wolves on the west coast were shot on sight as a matter of habit, an activity abetted by a provincial bounty right up to 1952. As a result, from about 1950 to 1970, it was thought that wolves might have been wiped out on Vancouver Island.

Cougars, too, were under threat by bounty hunters. One of the coast's best-known bounty hunters was Ada Annie Rae-Arthur—also known as Cougar Annie—who lived at the north end of Clayoquot Sound. According to a *Vancouver Sun* article in 1957, she shot sixty-two cougars and about eighty black bears during her years at Hesquiat Harbour. In 1955 alone, she killed ten cougars, earning $400 for her efforts.

Today, with the bounty long gone, predators have moved back into the Long Beach area and other parts of the west coast ecosystem. Sightings of wolves and cougars are not infrequent, though it is more common to see only their scat or tracks. Genetic testing shows that the lineage of the new wolf residents traces to the mainland. It appears that after the Vancouver Island wolves—a distinct subspecies of timber, or grey wolf—were wiped out locally, the central coast wolves moved over, likely by swimming across the narrows at the island's northern end.

Wolves travel throughout the west coast islands and beaches and often use Long Beach and the mudflats at Grice Bay as "travel corridors." Recent analysis shows that their diet is largely composed of deer, raccoon, river otter, and harbour seal. Salmon, clams, shore crabs, and occasionally even birds, bears, and berries, are also on the menu.

While the size of the wolf population is not clear, the cougar population is known to be high on Vancouver Island. (Its density is one of the highest recorded in the world.) Like the original population of wolves here, Vancouver Island cougars are also a unique subspecies.

Although our relationship with these predators can be an uneasy one, a healthy predator population is one indicator of a well-functioning ecosystem. Predators need a large territory and adequate prey. Long Beach and the forested lands around it satisfy only a portion of their needs. Local research has shown that wolves and cougars often hunt and travel shorelines for the variety of prey there. After the beaches are gated at night, animals have the run of the place. Their presence here certainly keeps the wild in wilderness.

be far enough away from race-meetings, clubs, Deauville and Monte Carlo not to be tempted to gamble." Ada and Violet did not accompany Ernest to Canada, but Ruth did.

By 1904, father and daughter were living in Victoria, where Ruth had some renown as an amateur singer. Four years later, Leverson had made his first Long Beach land investments, with a lot for himself as well as one each for his estranged wife and his children. It seems Ernest might not have changed his gambling ways, however, for when he died in 1922, his younger brother, David, held the mortgages on all of the Long Beach properties.

Like many others who bought land at Long Beach with the sole dream of turning a profit, it's doubtful that any of the Leversons ever visited their lots there, not even Ernest and Ruth while they resided in Victoria. Ada and Violet are thought to have never even visited Canada, period. Ada, after all, was far too busy leading a literary life in Europe. A novelist and frequent contributor to magazines of the day such as *Punch* and *The Yellow Book,* she had become a prominent figure in literary and artistic circles. While she chummed about with many writers, she is probably best known for being a dear and faithful friend to Oscar Wilde, who encouraged her writing and called her "Sphinx."

6

from working the land
to working the view

A<small>T SOME</small> time in the night, the power has gone out. The clock radio is blinking, and the surge protector on my computer backup battery is pinging away. We wake to a morning of pelting rain and howling winds, the latter no doubt responsible for taking down a power line somewhere in the area. No power means school will be cancelled and, with my computer on enforced recess, work might as well be cancelled, too. In the stormy days of winter, we have come to accept this occasional inconvenience and are prepared for it. Today, we have even planned to venture out into the elements for a hike. It's storm-watching season after all, and we know that many people come to Long Beach expressly to experience Nature's wrath exactly like today's wet and wild fury.

The stroke of marketing brilliance that turned what might otherwise have been considered a detriment—a winter season that is rainy, windy, and generally grey—into one of the area's major tourism selling points began in the early 1990s when park staff teamed with *Beautiful British Columbia* magazine to produce an article on the edgy allure of winter storms. The reprised Wickaninnish Inn, which opened in 1996 in Tofino, ran with the idea. The inn took a creative page from the Rumpelstiltskin tale, spinning wind and water into gold, when it began to promote storm watching to its guests. Now people come to the area from all over the world specifically because of the storms, purchasing specially designed storm-watching packages at the Wickaninnish Inn and other west coast resorts. Guests may be offered raingear and rubber boots when they arrive and even guided hikes out into the fray, though many will opt to view storms from indoors. After all, the main draw is the reckless romance of it, the mesmerizing power of waves meeting shoreline. Massages, soaker tubs, and champagne service with a view help, too.

Typical winter weather on the west coast is a steady march of low pressure systems across the Pacific. Since winds blow from regions of high pressure to those of low pressure, these systems bombard the coast with steady winds. Being able to roll unimpeded across a wide open Pacific also means that these winds often arrive packing stunning strength, sometimes up to hurricane force (greater than 118 kilometres, or 73 miles, per hour, the equivalent of 64 knots) and with the gargantuan waves to match. The lower the pressure the stronger the winds and the bigger the storm.

On this day, when we find ourselves resignedly powerless, the forecast is calling for Beaufort 7, meaning a "moderate" gale with winds up to sixty-one kilometres, or thirty-eight miles, per hour (thirty-three knots). We head to Long Beach, where the broad vista of galloping rollers is thrilling to watch. It's much safer here, too, than at smaller beaches. The sandy width at low tide gives us room to get off the beach before the surging seas reach the beach logs. Even modest waves can turn logs into deadly bludgeons. It's important to be wary of such dangers out here, every day really, but especially on days like this. It's rare, but people have been killed in the Long Beach area, usually swept from rocky headlands where, made bold by the weather's own devil-may-care antics, they submit to the prospect of an exhilarating sea-spray drenching and instead end up in the path of a mountainous wave. Our children know the mantra, "Never turn your back on the ocean." And on days like today, the ocean deserves our attention and respect.

It's exciting, but only to a point. Walking into the wind, we must keep our upper bodies bent low. Even so, the wily, gale-driven rain blasts at our cheeks as if it were sharp needles of ice. After an hour or so of hard trudging, we turn back toward the parking lot. The wind, now at our backs, shoulders us brutishly and sails us down the beach.

We bundle back into the car invigorated, our cheeks tingly and our noses runny. At moments like this, I wonder what some of the early tourists to Long Beach, those who came only in the summer, might have thought of this twenty-first-century attraction to storms. Would they see it as utter madness? Or would they completely understand?

A Destination Is Born

Long Beach's vacation potential didn't catch fire quickly, even as a summertime destination, partly because of the remote location and, tied to that, partly because of the relative rawness of its

A trip to Long Beach was a special treat for residents of Ucluelet, Tofino, and Clayoquot. Dorothy Abraham, from Tofino, wrote, "... we would spend the night on the beach, build a huge fire to keep the cougars away, bake potatoes and clams, and sleep in holes scooped in the sand." These visitors are taking in the view from Schooner Cove.

guest-support infrastructure: transportation, lodgings, supplies, and services catering to visitors were in their infancy. Despite the best efforts of the early tourism boosters, Long Beach was still not well known as a holiday spot. Nor was it easy to reach even from the nearby communities of Tofino, Clayoquot, and Ucluelet, let alone other areas of Vancouver Island. These realities dampened early flames, but there was no question that word about this mythical west coast paradise was filtering out.

Hand in hand, through the 1920s and 1930s, dogged promotion and gradual road improvements slowly but surely drove a shift in attitude about Long Beach both from within the community and from without. Gradually, "working the land" made room for "working the view."

The Jacksons' "House on the Hill"

One of the best records of the early days of tourism at Long Beach can be found in George Jackson's two journals. Jackson moved to the coast in 1924 to work as a lineman. He rented a house that sat on land that was first pre-empted by Walter Dawley and later became part of Charles Harvey's ranch. Jackson's wife, Lucy, and adult daughter, Gertrude, split their time between Victoria and Long Beach. Both Charles Harvey and Jacob Arnet had moved on by this time, but feral cattle still roamed the Burnt Lands, beach, and forest. Three horses and the Jacksons' own cattle grazed in the field in front of the house, where the Long Beach parking lots now sit. The Jacksons kept hens and had a large vegetable and flower garden. Jackson also hunted and foraged. His journals detail, with a gourmand's care, meals of venison, duck, wild mushrooms and cranberries, clams, fish, and occasionally even wild cattle.

Jackson maintained the telegraph line from Long Beach to South Bay, toward Tofino, and a spur line up to Cannery Bay, location of the Clayoquot Sound Canning Company. Because his home was a switchpoint on the line, it became a frequent stop of Long Beach settlers or passersby wanting to send a telegram, pick up their mail, or drop in for a chat, a cup of tea, a meal, or even a night's rest. For that last purpose, the Jacksons had erected two guest tents set on wooden platforms at the back of the house.

Between January 1, 1927, and May 22, 1929, Jackson made a journal entry almost every day. Most were terse—for example, "Rained all day" or "Johnnie Johnson dead in Victoria"—but all the bits collectively provide a detailed picture of life in the Long Beach area at the time. Jackson was a keen observer of his surroundings, noting not only the daily weather, growth of his cabbages, and laying prowess of his hens, but also the activities of his neighbours, including the native people who regularly came to their land at "Hesawista" (now Esowista) to gather clams and berries or hunt sea lions or deer. At times, he also reported snippets of news from town, received through passersby and through the calls or wires that came to his home. If any unfamiliar boats or people were in the area, Jackson noted that in his journal, too, acting as *de facto* border guard on the remote stretch of coastline. On April 19, 1927, for instance, he wrote, "Three American boats still anchored in behind Box Island, have been there five days now. Probably bootleggers waiting for Mother ship so they can load up." It's very likely they *were* bootleggers. Prohibition was in effect in the United States, and it was common knowledge that rum-runners were working off the west coast.

Within a couple of years of settling in at their Long Beach home, the Jacksons' guest book began filling up with entries

From his two-storey house on a slight rise above the beach and close to the trail to Mud Bay, George Jackson and his family had a panoramic view of Long Beach and all that went on there. Horses belonging to Jackson and his neighbours ran semi-wild on Long Beach.

Especially colourful among the many colourful settlers at Long Beach was Charlie Hughes, who pre-empted land there in 1925. Hughes was well known for his suit made of burlap sacking, his penchant for walking barefoot and wearing animal skins, and the house he shared with his beloved goats.

made by friends and tourists visiting from both ends of the peninsula. The most frequent callers were their friends the four Hillier brothers from Ucluelet, who came to the beach to hunt deer and waterfowl. Bill Hillier was the lineman from Long Beach to Ucluelet; Bert and Pete worked a trapline in the area (catching mostly raccoon and mink); and George Hillier ran a

The Hillier brothers were great friends of George Jackson and spent a lot of time at Long Beach where they would come to check their traplines and hunt deer or wild cattle.

fishing boat, the *Manhattan,* which he sometimes anchored down near Box Island and then popped up to the Jacksons for a visit.

The Hilliers were one of the first families to have a vehicle on the coast despite the dearth of passable roads. When they first received their car, they were happy enough to drive back and forth along a stretch of road in Ucluelet barely half a kilometre long. A car was a novelty in those days, so even a spin as limited as that was a source of amusement and interest. And the Hilliers, like most west coast residents then, held out hope that they would one day have local roads that they really could drive without fear of bogging down in muck or landing in a waist-deep mud hole. At least by 1923, they could drive the rough road that finally connected Ucluelet to Long Beach.

The Good Roads League and other area associations did not let up in their calls for an improved road, especially one that would link Ucluelet and Tofino. The group had a minor, if ironic, victory in 1926, when federal surveyors erected a sign near Tofino's village dock: the Pacific Terminus of the Trans-Canada Highway. In fact, Tofino's road petered out in the bush a few kilometres from town. And, as local resident Walter Guppy observed, "much of the road wasn't suitable for wheelbarrows or decently shod people."

The announcement foretold some break in the stonewalling, however, for in the summer of 1927, several road crews were indeed busy at work surveying, laying gravel, digging ditches, and measuring bridge sites. In the Depression era, road building provided relief work for unemployed men, mostly from the city. Several camps at Long Beach offered opportunities for men to work in exchange for relief wages (at times as low as 20 cents a day) or in lieu of paying taxes. Most of the men worked only with picks and shovels, which made for slow progress. Large machinery that was brought in helped, but even it was tested by the area's hardscrabble terrain. An entry in Jackson's journal in July 1927 reports the arrival of a five-ton tractor and grader, which in short order got stuck.

By August, the first vehicle to attempt the sixteen-kilometre (ten-mile) drive from Tofino to Long Beach set off. It was a government road truck, and it got just over the halfway point before being mired in the mud.

CARS, PLANES, AND A SUBDIVISION

In May 1927, Jackson learned that the ranch property he and his family had occupied for three years had been purchased by a Mr. Lovekin of Riverside, California. Word that the ranch at Long Beach was about to change hands meant that Jackson would have to move on, but he had time to plan. With his friend C.J. Ayliffe of Port Alberni, Jackson arranged to purchase a property that lay adjacent to the Hesawista (Esowista) Reserve.

The two men took possession in October 1928, and over the next months, Jackson, often with the help of Pete Hillier, worked on clearing sections of the land. Ayliffe and Jackson then sub-divided the property, which they, too, called Hesawista, and put the lots up for sale. (The first one, Jackson recorded in his journal, went to a George Anderson for $275.) The Jacksons also built a cabin on one of the properties, as did Pete Hillier, who received two lots in exchange for his help.

Settled into their new home, the Jacksons were soon host-ing visitors again. Indeed, with a road of sorts finally punched through the forest linking Tofino and Ucluelet to Long Beach, the family received more guests than ever. And any reference in the guest book to the matter of "The Road" now meant a road that would link Long Beach to Port Alberni, and thus to eastern Vancouver Island, which in turn would mean easier access to the mainland and beyond. Almost immediately, duelling values over the fate of Long Beach emerged. Two entries from the Jacksons' guest book illustrate the divide:

[A] Motor Road from Alberni to Long Beach. What the West Coast needs more than anything. *September 3, 1929*

I only hope that the road never gets through to Long Beach, otherwise the place will be cluttered with a lot of millionaires, hot-dog stands and chocolate bar papers. *September 6, 1929*

Most guests continued to write effusively about the beauty of the place (often moved to poetry), but in these new times, some people saw the beauty as secondary to the natural speedway the

The earliest cars on Long Beach came via Ucluelet. They were barged up Alberni Inlet and off-loaded at the dock. The beaches of Florencia Bay and Long Beach were part of the early "highway."

beach provided. ("A wonderful place to drive old Henry #9159 along at full speed," reads one message. "The finest beach I ever saw. A wonderful place for racing of all kinds," reads another.)

The family's journals and guest book also record several "firsts" for motorized tourists. The first "foreign car," as Jackson called it, on Long Beach was a new Dodge "closed in car" driven by John Alexander. Alexander had started his journey in Kalamazoo, Michigan, driving across the U.S. to California and then up into Canada, eventually reaching Port Alberni. From there, he shipped his car to Ucluelet and drove up to Long Beach, arriving there on July 19, 1927. The first motorcycle on the beach was ridden by Tom Scales and J.R. Tindall of Vancouver on August

THE FOG DAYS OF SUMMER

It is August, the last month of the summer holidays, and heat records may be falling daily in the rest of the province, even on eastern Vancouver Island, but not here on the west coast. While it's not a place particularly noted for summer heat, we do have sunny and warm days, even through the fall. However, it seems that just as summer begins to take hold at Long Beach, the days of "Fogust" roll in. The fleece jacket makes a comeback, at least in the morning until the fog burns off.

Although it can show up any time of the year, ironically it is in the late summer, just when the days have grown warmer and people's moods more carefree, that fog typically sneaks in as if hoping to break up the party. It forms when ocean breezes blow the warm, moist air from the Pacific over relatively cooler waters along the coastline. This causes the air to condense like warm breath does on a cool window. The fog further settles at the shoreline because of temperature differences between the land and sea. After days of warm temperatures, heated air above the land rises. The cooler, denser sea air flows in to fill the gap, drawing the fog along with it.

The sun's heat can usually burn light fog off by midday, but by the time temperatures cool by evening, the fog has usually returned. Heavy fog takes longer to dissipate and may last for days until winds are able to shuffle it off.

While it can be frustrating at times to sit in fog while the rest of the province enjoys the heat of summer, fog performs a valuable service in the west coast environment. Even if it doesn't rain for a period, the forest remains cool and the air moist because of the forest's ability to gather the fog's moisture. As fog condenses on the needles of coniferous trees, the water droplets fall to the ground. The soil, trees, and smaller plants store this moisture like a big sponge. Each evening, the respiring plants slowly release the collected moisture. In the summer of 2003, when Tofino's reservoir on Meares Island came perilously close to dry each day after heavy use, it filled every evening even though there had been no rain for over a month. That was thanks to fog and forests. Up to 35 percent of west coast precipitation actually comes from fog, not rain.

3, 1929, where the two had little trouble reaching speeds of 145 kilometres (90 miles) per hour. ("The finest speedway ever seen," they wrote in Jackson's guest book.) And the first two planes, flown up from San Francisco in a flying time of eight hours, landed on the beach on July 1, 1930.

A road, cars, motorcycles, planes, and a subdivision. In his few years at Long Beach, George Jackson had lived through a significant era of change, witnessing and even participating in developments. But he would see few others. Shortly after the departing planes taxied down the beach and took off in July 1930, Jackson also left for the last time. On September 3, 1930, at the age of sixty-three, he died in Victoria. A simple cross marks his grave in the Ucluelet cemetery.

The Donahues and Lovekins

George Jackson wrote about suspicious boats and rum-runners in his midst a few times in his journal. Had he still been alive and living at Long Beach in 1933, he would have had a rum-runner for a neighbour. That summer, Hazel and Jim Donahue moved to Long Beach. Hazel was raised in Tofino and had been visiting Long Beach all her life. During the days of prohibition in the United States, Hazel's brother, Stuart Stone, was a rum-runner and captain of the *Malahat,* AKA Queen of the Rum Fleet. Jim, who had sailed extensively throughout the world, worked on the *Malahat* for a time. Stuart introduced Jim to his sister, and the two married in 1931. Hazel had put a few hours into her brother's illegal liquor supply business, too. She was a long distance operator with BC Telephone, but at night she worked out of a Vancouver basement relaying messages to the rum fleet.

In the summer of 1933 (and prohibition now over), the Donahues arrived at Long Beach for a six-month holiday. They had

Jim and Hazel Donahue with Hazel's mother, Christene Stone, at their
Long Beach home. The Donahues originally came for six months but stayed
for more than twenty years. In time, they built more cabins and called their
establishment Camp Maquinna.

removed the back from their Model T Ford, loaded it with lumber
and camping supplies, and caught the steamer to Ucluelet. Initially, they had permission from the government's Indian Agent
to live on the native reserve at Esowista, but they later moved
farther down the beach toward Green Point, on the corner of the
land owned by the Lovekins. The spot was idyllic but not altogether free: they were charged a rent of 50 cents a month, except
in June, July, and August, when the rent jumped to $2 a month.

Hazel's mother, Christene Stone, lived with the couple at first.
Apparently, what Jim lacked in skills with a hammer and saw his
mother-in-law more than made up for. The large tent they built,
about five by eight metres (sixteen by twenty-six feet), soon had
a wood floor, partial wood walls, furniture, and a wood stove.

GIFTS FROM THE SEA

In the north Pacific, ocean currents cycle in immense gýres like water swirling in a wash basin. The Kuroshio and Oyashio Currents in the western Pacific merge to flow across the ocean in the Subarctic Current. This is slow motion movement: water can take two to five years to cross the Pacific, travelling about four to eight kilometres (two to five miles) a day. As it nears the coast of North America, this great river in the sea splits into the north-flowing Alaska Current and the south-flowing California Current. The physics of currents are complex and affected by localized subtleties. During the summer, for instance, a persistent counter-current moves against the prevailing surface current, flowing northwest and hugging the outer coast of Vancouver Island. At the same time, deep-water currents move in their own dynamic, driven by differences in ocean temperature and salinity.

For the beachcomber, currents serve as big conveyor belts, carrying and dropping off treasures and, soberingly, trash from the world's oceans. It is the cross-ocean currents that deliver one of the most sought-after treasures for a Long Beach beachcomber: glass balls. Lost by the fishing fleets off the Japanese coast, these floats can travel for years on ocean currents, their journeys only interrupted when storms drive the floats ashore.

Residents of Long Beach and the west coast have always looked to the sea as a sort of variety store. Milled lumber, cedar shakes, buckets, brooms, and occasionally even food in the form of ships' rations have all washed ashore over the years. More recently, lost cargoes of plastic toys, sports equipment, and Italian sandals have kept avid beachcombers busy.

When Prime Minister Pierre Trudeau visited Long Beach, he was given a classic west coast gift: a glass ball. The floats come from the nets of Japanese fishers and range in size from that of a small orange to a large beach ball.

Ultimately, even these treasures are really just garbage, cast or lost overboard. For years, they cycle in the Great Pacific Garbage Patch, a swath composed primarily of tonnes of plastic bits that cover an ocean area about twenty times the size of Vancouver Island. Much of this sort of plastic, mostly in small pieces, winds up on Long Beach or, worse, in the stomachs of sea birds that have mistaken the bits for food.

A.C. and Helen Lovekin's home, built overlooking Long Beach, became the extended family's summer residence for almost thirty-five years. The property included a large house, several small outbuildings, and substantial gardens. Today's Long Beach parking lots were once the fields in front of the Lovekin property.

Though not much larger than a small guest bedroom by today's standards, the Donahues' tent cabin obviously suited them perfectly, because their six-month vacation stretched into more than two decades of residency. They spent their days hunting, fishing, gathering clams and crabs, and endlessly beachcombing. Hazel later recounted some of the treasures they'd found: a wedding ring in a jar of buttons, dozens of bottles with a note inside, many glass fish floats, and, during the war, "rations all wrapped up in waxed paper—sausages in tins, cigarettes with little matches, candy, biscuits, lots of little plastic flashlights." Once, a little skiff washed in. They fished with that for years.

One day in 1936, the Donahues were joined in their paradise by a work crew that had come to build a summer home for the Lovekins, who, nearly ten years before, purchased the property George Jackson had rented. Although Jackson referred in his journal to Mr. Lovekin coming from California, Arthur C. ("A.C.") Lovekin had in fact been born and raised on a farm in Ontario and was again living part-time in Canada, in a home in Victoria. His wife, Helen, came from Boston. Lovekin was a successful businessman and over the years worked at a series of jobs and ran several enterprises in California, Hawaii (where he met Helen), and even Nelson, B.C., where, in 1895, he opened an assay office and did some prospecting.

When they bought the Long Beach property, the family had already explored parts of Vancouver Island, including Sproat Lake, where they spent the summer of 1921. It was then that A.C. got the notion of looking for land on the west coast of the island.

The newly built house was a far cry from the tent cabin that the Donahues had constructed and from any other homes on the beach. He hired a Victoria contractor, Robert Noble, who arrived at the beach with his wife, sons, and extended family to construct the substantial home. And unlike other Long Beach homes that had been built largely from logs or salvaged lumber, the Lovekin home used milled lumber. Peter Hillier used his fishing boat to deliver the boards to Long Beach, dumping the loads off on incoming tides. The construction crew gathered the lumber from the beach and wheeled it up to the building site.

Locally, their home was called the "Lovekin Estate," though the family never referred to it as such. When the work was completed, the property included a large main house, an annex with a bunkhouse and store room, and several small outbuildings to accommodate their family and friends who joined them at their coastal retreat for summer holidays. The arrival in town of the *Maquinna* with crates and barrels marked "china" or "glassware" destined for the Lovekin home only heightened the cachet surrounding this new kind of Long Beach resident: people who, though well accustomed to a certain level of luxury, were clearly as besotted by the beauty of the place as were their more modestly housed neighbours.

The Lovekins spent about six months a year at Long Beach. A.C. was seventy-four years old by the time the house was ready but still full of energy and enthusiasm that he poured into his new property. He created gardens and soaked up the beauty and glorious solitude. His children and grandchildren came to love the home as well.

The first year he came to live at the house, A.C. met the Donahues, and they quickly became friends. By the time the Lovekins moved back that fall to Victoria, the Donahues had been hired as caretakers of the Lovekin estate and remained so for many years.

The Whittingtons

The Lovekin house was still under construction when Peg and Dick Whittington bumped their way out to Long Beach in Peter Hillier's truck and off-loaded their crates. It was a beautiful sunny day in August 1936, and the young couple had arrived at their new home, a twenty-six-hectare (sixty-four-acre) lot just to the northwest of Green Point.

Times were tough everywhere in the 1930s, and the Victoria couple had been looking for a new direction. Dick first came out on foot, walking along a rough telegraph trail from Port Alberni to Kennedy Lake. There, he was met by a friend from the west coast, and the pair canoed down to the ocean and spent a few

Peg and Dick Whittington arrived at Long Beach in August 1936, and Peg lived at Long Beach for most of her adult life. She was casual about what they had accomplished, saying that she and Dick had simply worked hard and learned by trial and error—plus, if anything puzzled them, "there were always books."

days exploring Clayoquot and Tofino. On his return trip home via Ucluelet, Dick's route took him down Long Beach. Walking on the huge yet deserted beach, serenaded by the background rumble of waves hitting sand, he fell in love with the place. Back in Victoria, he approached Peg about the idea of making Long Beach their new home.

"We were looking for something and ready to leap at anything that was different than city living," Peg recalled years later. "Sure we argued it back and forth, pros and cons, and were we crazy or weren't we, but I was willing to give it a try."

From Working the Land to Working the View

The $300 the couple brought with them supported them for a year *and* financed the first house they built. They lived off the beach's plenty, dining regularly on clams, crabs, and salmon and supplementing that with flour, sugar, and other staples from town.

The Whittingtons' first task was to set up a camp. They put up their large canvas tent, moved their supplies in, and then grabbed their machetes. They had purchased the lot where Fred Tibbs had built his Tidal Wave Ranch. His house was still standing, higher up on the cliff above the beach. To get to it, the couple had to hack their way up through the wall of salal. It took three weeks. One of them would cut the brush and the other would clear it away. They found the single-room cabin in rough shape. At least twenty years had passed since Tibbs went off to build his islet castle near Tofino. The logs were rotten and wind blew through the walls, but the roof was sound. Dick and Peg cleaned it out, chinked the logs, and installed windows they'd hauled up the hill from the tent. The couple continued to sleep at the beach in the early days of their arrival, but once the cabin was ready, complete with a tiny tin stove, they moved in.

During the first year and a half, the Whittingtons chipped their home and livelihood out of the forest fronting Long Beach. They cleared an area large enough for a new house, dug a well, and put in a garden. Neither had homesteading experience, yet both were apparently well suited to it. They built their first house completely of wood they salvaged off the beach, mostly sawed lumber lost off the decks of passing ships. For the foundation they used rocks and creosoted posts, and for the roof, hand-cut shakes.

As with the Lovekins' place, the activity at the Whittingtons' property became a topic of curiosity and conversation. Any visitors to the beach made sure to stop by to see what they were up to. The locals, Peg assumed, figured it was only a matter of time before this brand of west coast living would get the better of the young pair.

"A lot of people came in and took a look because they wondered, 'Oh, these people won't stay. Nobody will stay there *that* long.'"

At the time, the beach was not considered a prime location or a smart investment. It was just too far from anywhere. Walking out to Tofino or Ucluelet along the rough trails could take three hours each way. Plus, it was a time when money was tight. Within a few years of the Whittingtons' arrival, for example, the property next door at Green Point was listed for $500, and nobody bought it. "There was no money," Peg recalled, "and [people saw] no future in the beach." It was a far cry from two decades earlier, when Tibbs had sold his land for $5,000.

From the start, Peg and Dick envisioned building a few cabins as holiday rentals. Once their own home was finished, they started in on building the guest cabins, working full tilt to get them up. A day off was considered a walk to beachcomb lumber. At first, the Whittingtons didn't have a name for their place, which they were reluctant to call a resort. Nevertheless, they ran a small newspaper ad in Victoria, and adventurous guests began trickling in, arriving by boat at Ucluelet and then getting a ride up to Long Beach. The guest book's first entry is dated July 1937.

People typically came for a week, maybe two, bringing all their own supplies. Each cabin had a stove, beds, and a few other basic items: "none of the luxuries, but all of the necessities," Peg liked to say. Every night after sunset there was a bonfire on the beach, and guests from the cabins gathered around the crackling driftwood to visit, while out beyond the circle of light the sound of distant breaking waves filled the dark. In time, the resort was named Singing Sands.

For a few years, most of the signatures in the Singing Sands guest book were from nearby residents—Hillier, Stone, Donahue, Lovekin—but slowly the guest range expanded, reaching to Port Alberni, Victoria, and beyond. Word was beginning to spread about a small resort out there on magnificent Long Beach.

In the summer of 1939, Edith Nelson paid a return visit to her old friends. On leaving, she wrote in the guest book, "Once more unto the beach, my friends." Whether intentional or not, her entry, playing on Shakespeare's "Once more unto the breach, dear friends" from *Henry v*, was portentous. *Henry v* opens just before the Battle of Agincourt begins during the Hundred Years' War. Not two months after Edith Nelson waved goodbye to the Whittingtons and headed home, Canada declared war on Germany.

Even on the remote western edge of Canada, things were about to change.

7

war comes to
long beach

IT'S EARLY morning in the bog, and as always the landscape
here has a fairy-tale feel, part sombre, part fanciful. Wafting
mist gives the yellow-cedars the look of gaunt watchmen lord-
ing over the bog's more diminutive neighbours, and the tufted
shore pines, resembling supersized heads of broccoli, add to its
whimsical nature.

I'm alone on my walk here today, which is usually just fine,
but thoughts of Sasquatch, said by some to roam this area near
Radar Hill and close to the golf course, stick in my mind like
small burrs. In one year, there were eight sightings, all from people very serious about what they saw. While there is not much
hard evidence of the 225-kilogram (500-pound) animal standing more than 2 metres (6 feet) tall, some west coast residents

117

are sure that the Sasquatch exists. Artist and author Emily Carr, describing Tsonoqua, a "wild woman of the woods" in First Nations mythology, wrote, "Half of me wished that I could meet her, and half of me hoped I would not." That pretty well sums up my feelings about the Sasquatch. It's the bog I've come to explore today, however, and I step carefully along the mucky trail trying not to look too hard for giant long footprints.

Like the mudflats, bogs are the misunderstood beauties of the west coast, relegated to backstage while all those centuries-old cedars, leaping whales, and vast expanses of fine sand bask in the spotlight. The dank bog reveals its beauty far more subtly and only to observers willing to look closely, possibly on their hands and knees.

All around me, I can see sphagnum mosses growing in pillowy profusion. If I sit down, the seat of my pants will be soaked through in short order. Moss's structure, with large empty cells, makes an ideal conduit for water. Some species can absorb twenty times their dry weight. It's for this reason that native people used sphagnum moss as absorbent pads, as did soldiers on Europe's battlefields to blot up everything from water to blood.

Not only do these mosses thrive in this saturated bog, but they also secrete organic acids that create the bog conditions. (Coastal streams are often the colour of tea. This is caused by tannic acid, one of the naturally occurring acids released by sphagnum.) An acidic habitat might sound like an unhealthy place to exist, but an entire complex of organisms is perfectly adapted to the boggy life. The yellow-cedar and shore pines stand highest here, and some individuals can grow for centuries. Still, these twisted and stunted trees only ever achieve a fraction of the size of their forest-dwelling relatives. Beneath the trees, Labrador tea, bog cranberry, crowberry, and bog laurel sit atop the mossy hummocks where they gain slightly better drainage. Lowest to the ground are the bog jewels: the tiny sundews and butterworts, whose petite daintiness belies their carnivorous appetite, as they lure and trap insects with sticky fluids. In the nutrient-poor environment, being a carnivore is a perfect way to get a meal.

No west coast bog is complete without the brilliant yellow of skunk cabbage, which grows in clumps in the muckiest part of the bog. Most flowers in the forests near Long Beach are relatively small and understated. Not so the skunk cabbage. In the spring, just when I start thinking the rains have gone on for far too long, the appearance of these brilliant yellow "swamp lanterns" rising out of the mire gives me hope that warmer days are on their way. The yellow "flower" of this plant is really a bract that partially hoods a spike covered in tiny greenish-yellow bumps, the actual flowers. The bract acts like a cloak around the spike of flowers, trapping whatever warmth the plant generates. This warmth also hastens diffusion of the skunk cabbage's distinctive funky odour. While other plants evolved sweet scents to attract pollinators, the skunk cabbage favoured putrid as the best scent to entice its preferred suitors, beetles and flies. More intriguing still is the evolutionary refinement effected by the plant, which releases not just one putrid odour but a range of them, each scent triggered for release by different temperatures and each known to be the best lure for the particular pollinator out at that time of day.

The acidic environment means that little decays in the bogs. The living mosses are actually the green tip of a layer of moss that could be several metres thick, with the compressed moss on the bottom (the peat) being several centuries old. This also means that bogs are perfect history books, trapping and preserving pollen and seeds in layer after layer that scientists can later "read" for clues about past climate and environment conditions. And who knows? Maybe deep down in this acidic, anoxic moss lies the preserved body of a Sasquatch, our own west coast bog man.

I carry on down the trail toward a drier spot where I'll stop for some lunch. Not far from here is the spot where Canso A 11007 crashed on February 10, 1945. The survivors spent hours nearby waiting for rescue, no doubt grateful to be alive and thanking their lucky stars that the plane sputtered and crashed near the relatively open landscape of a bog. The plane, locally referred to as "The Bomber," still sits where it ended its last flight over sixty years ago, its nose against a rocky outcropping and tail suspended metres above the forest floor. Its presence is a striking reminder of the big changes that the World War II era left on the Long Beach landscape.

The First Ripples of War on Long Beach

A romantic holiday cut short was Long Beach's first casualty of World War II. A young couple was staying at Singing Sands for their honeymoon. The groom had a small radio and was listening on September 10, 1939, when the announcement came that Canada had declared war on Germany. Being a naval reservist and fiercely loyal to the cause, he prepared to leave immediately. Resort owner Peg Whittington tried to talk some sense into him, suggesting he at least finish his honeymoon. She could only convince him to stay a few more days, though, as his patriotism exceeded his passions.

In the early months of World War II, Long Beach residents passed the days much as they always had. Coming out of the Depression was a slow business for west coast communities.

Work was scarce and intermittent, but with a bit of effort, food was plentiful. Clams, crabs, fish, waterfowl, venison, the bounty from backyard gardens, and perhaps a cow or coop of chickens all kept food on the table.

At the time, the population of this coastal area, including that of the native communities, was still well below one thousand. Forming a large part of the population of both Ucluelet and Tofino were Japanese-Canadians who had first arrived to fish in the early 1920s. By 1923, about ninety Japanese families had settled on the west coast: twenty-five in Tofino, six at Clayoquot, fifty in Ucluelet and the rest in Bamfield down the coast. (For a time, there were a few families near Long Beach, too, living in houses at Grice Bay.) By the 1930s, they were well established in all the communities.

Even before Canada entered World War II, the military had been present in the Long Beach area. Although much of the activity was focused on the Atlantic, the need to ramp up military presence on the west coast became evident as well. In October 1936, Ucluelet was chosen as the location of one of a series of "flying boat" stations along the Pacific coast. From a defensive standpoint it was an ideal choice. Ucluelet Harbour was relatively protected and situated near the entrance to Barkley Sound; it was close to the United States; and it helped protect the vulnerability of the Alberni Inlet, through which any successful enemy invader would gain a straight shot from Port Alberni over Vancouver Island to the mainland.

By late spring 1940, servicemen in the #4 Bomber Reconnaissance Squadron were relocated to their new base in Ucluelet. Living conditions at the time were grim. The construction crew arrived barely ahead of the squadron, essentially building the station around them.

The Enemy, Weather

As the war progressed, concern over a seaborne invasion of the west coast grew and establishing airfields rose on the priority list. Air force officials began searching for locations to build airports that could support land-based fighter and bomber aircraft squadrons. After a lengthy reconnaissance and surveying, the Burnt Lands adjacent to the Lovekin home was chosen as the site of the new Royal Canadian Air Force Station Tofino. (The Lovekins donated land for a military hospital, and some Tla-o-qui-aht families living near Esowista were also asked to lend their land for the cause. The Lovekins' land was returned to them after the war. The natives' land was absorbed into the airport.)

A more challenging building site could hardly have been picked. With no road access from Port Alberni, construction equipment and the huge number of skilled tradesmen required to build the base had to come by water. Just housing and feeding the crews would be a logistical challenge. Still, the air force forged ahead, determined that Long Beach was the best spot. Engineers inspected the proposed airport site in May 1941, and just five weeks later, two barges arrived at Ucluelet loaded with heavy equipment and lumber for the new airport.

It was clear from the start that the toughest enemies on the coast were going to be the weather and the geography. The wet days of winter were on their way, and much of the airport site selected was boggy and poorly drained.

The first order of business was to improve the road from Ucluelet to the Long Beach site and to prepare the airport building site. The successful contractor, Coast Construction Company, wallowed in the mud for weeks trying to clear away a sizeable patch of forest and scrub. With understaffed crews and bulldozers that bogged down repeatedly in the saturated land, progress was exceedingly slow—until December 7, 1941, and Japan's attack on the American base at Pearl Harbor. Practically overnight, the Long Beach air base project shot to the top of the RCAF's to-do list. Local workers, contracted to prepare a camp for the airport construction crew, cleared the long-abandoned homestead of August Arnet at McLean's Point in Grice Bay, even reclaiming the house and boathouse from thickets of salmonberry and alder.

Within a few weeks, the area thrummed with activity as construction crews moved in to occupy the site. The first task was to build a wharf at Grice Bay for gravel barges and then to push a nearly two-kilometre (one-mile) road through from the bay to the airport site. Tofino's Walter Guppy later recalled the activity in Grice Bay in the spring of 1942: strings of barges were towed into Grice Bay, filled with gravel dredged from the Cypre River. From there, a fleet of trucks hauled the gravel inland, where "bulldozers were stirring up a sea of mud in an attempt to remove the forest cover and level the area where the airport would be constructed." To the rescue charged Gordon Gibson, self-professed "Bull of the Woods." Coast Construction Company subcontracted Gibson to clear the land of all trees, stumps, and brush. He was well acquainted with clearing land on the west coast and transferred this logging knowledge to the airport site, using spars and donkey engines to remove the trees and shrubs. With that done, Coast Construction returned to level the ground, and airport construction began.

Before they pulled out, though, Gibson's crew was hired for one more job. Fears had arisen that Japanese planes might use Long Beach as a natural landing strip or as a place to launch a land assault. As a defensive solution, the RCAF contracted Gibson and his crew to drive lines of pilings into the sand from the high

Pilings driven along the length and width of Long Beach, and linked with barbed wire, were erected as a deterrent against an enemy invasion from the sea. Years after the war ended, the pilings were used as impromptu rally courses for drivers on the beach.

tide line all the way to the water's edge, down the entire length of the beach. Barbed wire and cables strung between the pilings in each line completed the deterrence.

Farewell to Friends

December 7, 1941, was a turning point in the war but also a pivotal point in the history of the Long Beach area. As soon as news of the Japanese bombing of Pearl Harbor hit the airwaves, Canada was considered to be at war with Japan, and RCAF Station Ucluelet went on active war alert. Security was heightened at the base with blackout conditions at night and dawn-to-dusk patrols. Air force personnel carried steel helmets and gas respirators at all times. Within days, Western Air Command sent 67 men to guard the Ucluelet base, and they were soon joined by 190 soldiers from the Royal Canadian Army. The influx of men strained the already-crowded base, where construction crews were still scrambling to finish building the facilities. By the end of that year, less than a month after the attack at Pearl Harbor, 32 officers and 400 men of other ranks called the RCAF Station Ucluelet home.

Meanwhile, the political climate for the area's residents of Japanese descent began to strain. On January 14, 1942, the Government of Canada declared all Japanese in Canada to be enemy aliens. On the west coast, rumours began to circulate: the Japanese school held on Saturday mornings was really military training; a Japanese man was just a bit too chummy with the airmen in Ucluelet; secret messages were being sent from basement hideouts or fishing boats. The truth was clouded by fear and confusion. Sadly, that made no difference in the end to the fate of the Japanese-Canadians on the west coast.

In January 1942, more than two dozen military and provincial police officers arrived and went door to door removing the telephones of Japanese residents. In March, the Canadian government ordered all people of Japanese descent to prepare to leave their homes within twenty-four hours. The station diary at RCAF Station Ucluelet recorded that on March 19, 1942, the *Maquinna* took away the last of the area's banished Japanese residents. Practically overnight, dear and longtime friends were supposed to have become enemies.

Forty years later, Islay MacLeod of Tofino reminisced about the departure: "Time seemed to stop for me that day... There were my friends, Emiko and her sister, Sachiko... and there was the Japanese boy who had won a place in my heart forever by helping me with my Arithmetic. And there were all the others milling about on the Government wharf... I had never seen so many Japanese adults and children together at one time. It seemed to my young eyes that half the population of Tofino was leaving. And there we were, the other half... watching as our former friends gathered their pitifully few belongings together."

RCAF Mudville

If clearing the RCAF Tofino site hadn't been difficult enough, constructing the airport buildings and fifteen-hundred-metre- (five-thousand-foot-) long runways notched up the challenge several times over. To build the runways, for example, a concrete plant had to be built first on the airport site. Even basic services such as water and electricity had to be established from scratch. The airport project was supposed to be top secret, but local residents could hardly ignore the hundreds of men flooding through their communities en route to the construction camp near Grice Bay. By now, the number of work crews living in a vast sea of shacks had ballooned, and the camp formed one of the largest villages on the coast.

While the construction crews worked maniacally, the RCAF was busy preparing squadrons for its newest base. Both #132 Fighter Squadron and #147 Bomber Reconnaissance Squadron trained on the mainland throughout the summer, waiting for their orders and assignment to the Tofino station. Finally, on October 14, 1942, Coast Construction sent word that the base was ready to receive the airmen.

The christening of the first of the three runways to open was not an auspicious beginning. The single-engine Lysander circled above Wickaninnish Bay, aimed at the airport, and began its descent over the beach logs. The plane touched down, veered out of control, and skidded off the runway. No one on board was injured, but the plane had to be barged to Vancouver for repairs.

Performance improved the next day when the #132 Fighter Squadron landed, but the euphoria of that success wore off almost before the engines had cooled as it became apparent that the reports of the base's state of readiness were wildly overblown. No buildings were ready to accommodate or feed the airmen, so they had to bunk in with the construction crew or live in tents. Then, when they were finally sent to their new barracks, they found a two-storey shell of a building with no interior partitions, no electricity, and no water (and thus no toilets, washing facilities, or showers). For heat, the men relied on a few wood-burning stoves whose chimney pipes were poked out a nearby window. The officers set up their quarters in an unfinished washroom that still had the piping for the toilets and sink protruding through the floor and walls. It was not a happy introduction to the area's wet and windy climate.

The situation with the airport facilities wasn't much better. Only the east-west runway had been completed. The other two were still riddled with tree stumps. There were no hangars for the planes or crew buildings. Planes sat at the edge of the runway, and ground crews shivered in small tents trying to stay out of the persistent rains.

Within two weeks, RCAF brass conceded the snafu. Desperate to speed things along, they issued orders for the airmen to be assigned to construction duties. As one of those men, Les Hempsall, later recalled, "From then on, fifty airmen of varying skills and experience in cooking, accounting, administration, stores, armament and aircraft maintenance reported daily to the construction superintendent with hammers and saws but with no knowledge of how to use them." Add to that the fact that the men had not been relieved of their regular jobs, and it is little wonder their efforts only added to the chaos. When the unionized construction workers rebelled and went on strike, the plan was quickly shelved.

Progress was, nevertheless, being made in staggering steps. On October 31, 1942, Hempsall wrote how there was "joy in Mudville" that night when Coast Construction Company finally hooked up two electric lights, one for the airmen's mess and one in the officers' mess. A month later, he wrote that the barracks had at last got hot and cold running water, "just in time for the pipes to freeze." By year's end, 6 toilets were newly installed, a bonus for the 387 men celebrating New Year's Eve at RCAF Base Tofino that year, if each man didn't mind standing in line with about 63 others to take advantage of the new luxury.

When spring came and the weather improved, Coast Construction accelerated operations in a final drive to get the job finished, bringing in five hundred more workers. Finally, by mid-1943, the barracks, mess hall, and a recreation hall were completed, and construction of the first hangar began.

So Little to Do and So Many to Do It

The Lovekins' guest book during the war years provides a glimpse into just how much activity was going on at Long Beach. Men from the Winnipeg Light Infantry, #4 Bomber Reconnaissance Squadron, 33rd Anti-Aircraft Battery, 1st Dufferin and Haldimand Rifles, 2nd Canadian Scottish Regiment, and even the Canadian Dental Corps all dropped in for a visit and a cup of coffee, hosted by the Donahues if the Lovekins were not in residence. No doubt these visits to a comfortable home were a welcome break to the men's monotonous routine. Air force squadrons patrolled

SHIFTING SEAS OF SAND

Tucked just above Long Beach, the rolling sand dunes at the south end of Long Beach have always been a draw. First Nations people came here, a place they called *tl'atl'athis*, to gather the glossy red fruit of kinnikinnick, or bearberry, that grows from the bush's long thin branches snaking across the sand. They usually stored the berries for later use, for instance, stirred into fermented salmon eggs. The grey beach peavine, an extremely rare plant with significant populations only in the dunes at Long Beach and on Graham Island in Haida Gwaii, also grows here. Other rare plants, such as the beach carrot and beach morning glory, add dashes of colour to the buff sandscape.

When I come here, I like to scramble up the steep bank at the back of the dunes. It rises to a knife-edge ridge, the back sloping to the forest below. Not that the bank is all that visible on this side. The salal is so thick you can hardly see the ground. One misstep could send you tumbling like Alice into a Wonderland tunnel of green. From the safe position atop the ridge, however, the view seaward is panoramic. This is a great spot for watching spouting grey whales in the spring. And sitting tall about a kilometre offshore is *tukwnit,* or Sea Lion Rocks. Native people used to paddle out there to hunt the seals and sea lions that haul themselves up onto the rocks to rest.

At the base of the dunes, the wind sometimes fingers away the sand to expose shards of metal, litter left from the firing range set up here during World War II or even from the New Year's Day trap shoots once held annually on the dunes by Long Beach locals. Military survival camp exercises, motorcycle antics, impromptu target practice by those sober and drunk—the dunes have endured much pernicious use over the last half-century. Today, they are quiet, visited only by the occasional hiker and serving as an important travel corridor for animals, including wolves, cougars, and bears.

In the past, conventional thinking was that dunes needed to be stabilized to be preserved and to protect coastal buildings and infrastructure. Today, restoration science suggests the opposite is true. Sand and the dunes they create are naturally mobile because of the wind; by

During World War II, training exercises broke up the monotony of life on the base. As part of the men's training, the air force held survival camps in the sand dunes at the south end of Long Beach. Dune ecosystems are rare in British Columbia, which makes Long Beach's dunes especially significant.

encouraging and allowing that mobility, we can better preserve these vulnerable ecosystems.

It is the dynamic nature of dunes that keeps them complex and richly diverse. As their very substrate moves about, so do nutrients and plant communities. If the sand stops moving, plants on the dune's edges—mosses and trees such as spruce and cedar—can gain a foothold and start encroaching on the dune, ultimately ruining the habitat and its inherent "dune-ness." In the Long Beach sand dunes, national park biologists are working to remove a different problem: invasive European beach grass. This species of dune grass was commonly planted elsewhere in the 1940s as a way to anchor dunes. Although not purposely introduced at Long Beach or even on Vancouver Island, partial plants, with roots intact, found their way here anyway, carried by the wind and ocean, and today European beach grass has a stranglehold on the dunes. Removing this grass by hand and by backhoe helps restore the natural cycles of change on the dune.

the coast on twelve-hour flights reaching eight hundred kilometres (five hundred miles) out to sea, searching for submarines and
monitoring activity in the shipping lanes.

The air force squadrons were soon joined by army personnel
tasked with protecting the base. Four army camps were positioned between Tofino and Ucluelet, including one at Schooner
Cove. The soldiers worked out of bunkers hidden among the
beach logs and covered by sand. Over at McLean's Point, on Grice
Bay, another contingent guarded the fuel-storage tanks, and gun
positions were scattered throughout the area. A corps of Royal
Canadian Engineers wired the airstrip for demolition in case of
attack.

Training for both the air force and army was ongoing and
helped break the monotony of waiting for an enemy that, in the
end, never arrived. A rifle range and survival school was set up in
the Long Beach sand dunes; an obstacle course was run along an
abandoned road cutline near McLean's Point; mock attacks were
staged; and men practised their survival skills in the bush, fash-
ioning shelters from driftwood and parachutes and hunting and
fishing for food.

Still, they often had time on their hands. For many, this was
a posting to a remote, muddy hellhole, and amazingly there were
some men who only ever flew over Long Beach and never set
foot on it during their whole time stationed on the coast. Others,
however, wandered down whenever they had the opportunity
to take a quick dip, hike along the rocky headlands, or join in a
game of baseball or rugby. Because there were no married quarters on the base, the Whittingtons, and the Donahues to a lesser
extent, rented cabins to wives and families of servicemen for
about $15 a month. Both the Whittingtons and Donahues also
allowed a few of the men to build cabins on their properties,

The wooden shacks at Pacific Heights, or "Dog Patch," changed hands for about $75 as servicemen and their families came and went from the makeshift community.

providing the men with the materials in return for their labour and a place for their families to live while they were posted to the coast. Other servicemen housed their wives and families in shacks moved from the air base construction camp to Schooner Cove in a makeshift community called Pacific Heights. With outside toilets and no electric lights or running water, these accommodations were very basic, but the setting more than made up for that.

The flood of people, mostly young men, brought change and excitement to the area. "The boys," as Peg Whittington called them, "cheered things up a lot." There were dances and picnics, whist drives and other fundraisers for the war effort both in Ucluelet and Tofino.

The air base at RCAF Base Tofino dramatically changed the landscape of the Long Beach area, literally and figuratively. During its short operation, the base was the largest community on the west coast. This photograph shows #147 Bomber Reconnaissance Squadron ground crew on a Bolingbroke Bomber. Note the impressive hangar, one of two at the base.

At the end of the summer of 1944, Secret Order #304 closed RCAF Station Tofino less than 2 years after the first plane landed on the runway. At its height, the station housed more than 1,100 personnel, and hundreds more lived in the army camps surrounding the station. To anyone who had been absent for those 2 years and only returned to the area then, it would have looked as though a town had fallen intact from the sky into the old bog-and-forest landscape below. Almost 50 buildings of various sizes were left at war's end, including 2 airplane hangars, a 128-bed hospital, a 2-chair dental clinic, a recreation hall, a canteen and 13-bay garage, bomb and pyrotechnic stores, barracks, and mess halls.

The base didn't completely shut down, however. In November, it became a Signals Unit with fewer than two hundred personnel. No aircraft or aircrew remained, but pilots from other bases flew out to the coast and used the airstrips to practise takeoffs and landings. The airport was serving in that function when RCAF Canso #11007 from Coal Harbour on northern Vancouver Island landed at Tofino on the afternoon of February 10, 1945, for a short stop to practise on the runway and test repairs on their port engine.

At 11 P.M., with 12 people, four 250-pound depth charges, and a full load of fuel onboard, the plane departed. Shortly after takeoff, the port engine spluttered and died. The pilot, Ronnie J. Scholes, tried to turn back to the airfield to no avail. With the plane quickly losing altitude, Scholes pulled the plane into a full stall to slow it down. It hit near the bottom of a hill, breaking through trees and standing almost tail up before finally crashing down. All the lights were out, and one crewman later recounted hearing a crackling noise over the dead silence aboard. Looking forward, he saw the port engine on fire and a waterfall of gasoline pouring from the ruptured left wing tank.

Miraculously, all twelve passengers survived. Scholes had a fractured forehead and a broken nose, eight people had minor cuts and bruises, and the remaining three were unhurt. They all crawled out of the wreck and hiked down to the flats below. Help wasn't long in coming. When the Canso hadn't arrived at Coal Harbour as scheduled, a search plane set out to look for them. Once located, the crew was hiked out.

After the downed crew's rescue, a second RCAF team went to the crash site to retrieve the radios and machine guns. They also removed and detonated the depth charges a few hundred metres from the wreck. Today, a perfectly circular pond about ten metres (thirty feet) across fills the crater blasted out by explosions. Every spring, the pond grows thick with the egg masses of Northwestern salamanders, each a grapefruit-sized ball of clear jelly.

SPLAT

While the improved highway at Long Beach may have made travel easier for humans, it did just the opposite for the area's frogs, salamanders, and newts, whose travel corridors took them blindly across the highway during their migrations. Thanks to the work of local volunteers on a project affectionately referred to as SPLAT (Society for the Prevention of Little Amphibian Tragedies or Some Poor Little Amphibians Trampled), the extent of amphibian carnage has been greatly reduced. Today, small fences erected along the Long Beach highway in several locations bisect migratory routes of the local amphibians, stopping them before they reach the treacherous road surface and directing them to a tunnel under the highway.

The damp environment of the west coast is perfect for frogs and salamanders, including tree frogs, the rough-skinned newt, the Northwestern salamander, the Western red-backed salamander, the wandering (cloud) salamander, and the red-legged frog, which is a federal "species of concern." The bogs, ponds, and ditches of the Long Beach area are excellent amphibian breeding patches. Add to that endless moist terrestrial habitat well stocked with decaying logs and forest leaf litter, and amphibians have the perfect homes-away-from-water, with an abundance of insects and other small invertebrates to feed on.

The presence of amphibians helps biologists assess the ecological integrity of the area, since these small animals are some of the first to be affected by changes in the environment, including air and water quality. They are the west coast's "canary in a coal mine" and are monitored by counts of adults (alive and dead) and their egg masses, which can reach impressive size. A female red-legged frog can lay more than a thousand eggs at a time in a jelly-like mass that looks like a cluster of grapes. The Northwestern salamander's egg mass holds dozens of pea-sized eggs.

Northwestern salamanders are common residents of the forests and wet-lands of the Long Beach area. They breed and lay their eggs in water and spend their adult lives in the forests, often underground or in decaying logs.

Listening to calls is another way to monitor amphibians. No one at Long Beach, human or native amphibian, ever wants to hear the *bwum, bwum, bwum* of the American bullfrog, whose accidental introduction to habitats on southern Vancouver Island has spelled catastrophe for indigenous species. It's truly a bully of a frog, eating other amphibians and out-competing them for habitat. To date, the Long Beach area has remained bullfrog-free, and the hope is that it will stay that way.

If the leading edge of the cloud that was about to sweep over Long Beach during World War II was signalled by a truncated honeymoon, perhaps it was fate that saw the need to mark the cloud's departure with another casualty of the heart.

In March 1946, a large mine floated onto the beach near Dick and Peg Whittington's Singing Sands resort. They reported it to George Redhead, the provincial policeman stationed in Ucluelet, who in turn sent word to the Canadian navy. Although Redhead advised them to land at Ucluelet, from where he would drive the detonation crew out to the beach site, the navy insisted on proceeding by sea straight out to Green Point and sending the men ashore in a small boat. Redhead and the Whittingtons knew this was a foolish decision—launching and rowing through the surf was risky at the best of times and even more so in the late winter's high seas—but they had little say in the matter.

Offshore, a skiff with five men was lowered, and they headed in. They made it safely to the beach and set about exploding the mine. The plan went awry, however, when the men tried to return to the base ship. As they strained at the oars to propel the small boat through the breakers, they were flipped over into the churning surf. Dick and Redhead raced in to help while Peg ran to the house for rope. When she got back, she could see three of the navy men struggling in the surf as another clung to the overturned skiff and the fifth was trying to gain purchase on the rocks off the beach. Eventually, three of them were rescued and brought to shore, and Peg and a neighbour drove the shaken men to Singing Sands to warm up.

Dick, meanwhile, had with great difficulty made it onto the rocks of Green Point to help the stranded sailor still in trouble there. Whether Dick was swept into the water by the wave surge

Dick Whittington (L) and George Hillier (R) with an unexploded mine Whittington discovered on Long Beach. The navy expedition sent to detonate the mine ended in tragedy.

or pulled in by the man he was trying to save is not clear, but Dick disappeared. Only later was his body found down the beach toward Sandhill Creek. One of the naval men also drowned in the incident.

Dick was posthumously awarded a medal for his part in the rescue. Peg chose not to go to the ceremony; instead his mother accepted the medal.

"Everybody thought I should leave the beach after that," Peg said years later, "and I thought I shouldn't."

8

unknown no more

IN THE summer months at Long Beach, we've come to expect
that many of our visitors will be keen to have at least one feast
of Dungeness crab, a seafood for which the area is well known.
We're only happy to oblige. Unless we've had time to go out in our
boat and set the crab trap, we do the next best thing: head to the
house of a local fisherman when the red crab-shaped for sale sign
is out. Either way, I'm always reminded of tales of the days when
crabs were so plentiful that people used *rakes* to scrape crabs out
of the tide pools at Long Beach.

One of the most popular spots for catching crab in the past
was the Great Tide Pool at the south end of the beach, today near
the park interpretive centre. It seems that everyone staying at
the beach, whether in a resort or camping or squatting nearby

at Wreck Bay, made the trek to the pool when they had a hankering for crab and wanted easy take-out. Today, it is rare to find any Dungeness crab in that tide pool. Still, there is much life to see there and in the other tide pools at Long Beach and all along the west coast's rocky shores.

When the tide is out, tide pools provide vital refugia—literally, refuges—ideal marine "safe houses" for intertidal animals that can't tolerate air exposure and changes in temperature or salinity very well.

In tide pools, the line between plants and animals is, at least superficially, blurred. Vibrant green "flowers" are really sea anemones, a marine invertebrate whose chubby petal-like tentacles capture food. Crusty-looking barnacles, which seem as inert as the rocks they affix to, also come alive when covered with water, their shrimp-like animal selves sending out feathery cirri to fan the water for food. Even the walls of tide pools are covered in life. The bubblegum-pink splashes are coralline algae, and the scarlet swatches are a type of sponge, also an animal. Nothing moves too quickly in a tide pool with the exception of sculpins, well-camouflaged fish that dart about like tiny Cold War spies in a B movie. Sit quietly and you might also see a small shell edge sideways as a hermit crab shuffles on, or the spine of a sea urchin rotate in its socket, or a sea star slip, almost imperceptibly, lower into the water. Predator, prey, herbivore, carnivore, scavenger—each member of a tide pool plays a role in maintaining that community's balance.

It's hard not to observe a tide pool and see a perfect mini-community, appealing in its apparent orderliness and completeness, at least for that moment. Both time and tide inevitably bring change, however. Sometimes it is subtle. A change in temperature after a series of hot days might be the demise of one species, upsetting the balance of who eats whom and how often. Adjustments are made. Sometimes the change is wrought much more harshly and without warning, like when the sharp claws of a rake scour repeatedly through the tiny landscape or cars race through or fighter planes strafe the waters. Adjustments are also made then, but not without casualties.

In fact, the day-to-day interactions in a tide pool community are constantly shifting in relation to outside influences. In that respect, they are not all that different from human communities.

The Post-War Tourism Vanguard

The intense period of activity during World War II considerably stirred the waters of community life at and near Long Beach. With the war over, the normal course of daily business resumed, but with a difference.

Fishing and forestry breathed life and wages into Tofino and Ucluelet, but now there was a nascent third sector taking form. The early seeds of a tourism trade planted and fussed over for more than five decades had rooted with the hint of finally bearing fruit. It helped that a good percentage of the more than one thousand servicemen and civilians who had "discovered" Long Beach were spreading the word about this stellar holiday destination. One reality remained, however, to thwart those with visions of a burgeoning tourist trade: there was still no simple or direct access to the island's west coast. The August 12, 1949, issue of *Island Events* magazine, for example, ran an article called "Long Beach Beckons," describing Peg Whittington's "famous resort," Singing Sands. All you had to do to get there, the writer added, was to go to Port Alberni by car, bus, or train, take the MV

Guests to the Singing Sands resort at Long Beach would be met at the bus by Peg Whittington, her dog Posh, and her pony Duchess, who would pull the guests' luggage to the resort in a cart.

Uchuck from there out to Ucluelet, travel by bus from Ucluelet to Long Beach, and then walk from the drop-off down to Singing Sands. Peg would collect the luggage from the bus with her horse and cart.

Certainly this kind of adventure wasn't to everyone's liking, but Long Beach's appeal to a growing number of the holidaying public, regardless of the challenges to get there, showed no signs of abating. It was almost twenty years since the Donahues and the Whittingtons had first pitched their respective tents at the beach and then gone on to establish their own resorts. As demand for accommodation mounted during the summer, Camp Maquinna and Singing Sands soon saw more company.

WICKANINNISH LODGE

One of the first couples to add to Long Beach's resort selection were Nellie and Joe Webb. The couple moved from Duncan on eastern Vancouver Island "up and over the mountains" to the west coast in the late 1940s. The Webbs conceived of a resort that stressed comfort and friendliness over "fashionableness." They bought the property tucked into the southeast end of Wickaninnish Bay and drew up plans for their new business. They envisioned a modest camp with a cluster of simple cabins where, in such a beautiful setting, little embellishment would be necessary. At Wickaninnish Lodge, imagined the Webbs, visitors could escape their city-weary lives to stroll the vast beach, gaze into tide pools, relax by the fire with a book, or stare out the window all day if they so chose.

The couple acquired a section of the hospital building from the air force base in Tofino after it closed, moving the structure to their site and turning it into the main lodge. In time, they added a few small cabins. Visitors to the resort could rent housekeeping cottages for $25 a week or purchase an "American plan" package, with the resort providing all the meals. A single room in the lodge, with all meals, went for $45 a week. Nellie's mother, Mrs. Kerr, helped in the kitchen and won over many a visitor with her fine meals and even finer pastries. Of the Webbs, Joe was the more social, always willing to chat with guests. Nellie, though pleasant, always seemed to be working. With her power saw ("Wee MacGregor") and her horse (Punch) attached to a small cart, she was a regular sight up and down the beach, cutting firewood or gathering seaweed for the lodge's large garden.

The gracious personal touch of the hosts, the comfortable cabins on the Pacific's doorstep, and the memorable meals combined to rapidly earn the Webbs a devoted clientele who returned year after year.

Notable among those were Group of Seven artist Arthur Lismer and his wife, Esther. They spent their first summer at the resort in 1951, rebooking the same cabin for sixteen more years after that. The six weeks they installed themselves annually at Long Beach were a precious time for the Lismers and, as Canadian art historian Dennis Reid writes, the coast was an ideal retreat for the famous artist, being "perfectly suited to the increasingly personal nature of his painting, which was dependent upon an intense and intimate familiarity with natural forms."

Many Long Beach residents today still remember Lismer sitting with his paint box or sketch pad, walking along the beach or swimming. At the end of their holiday each summer, the Lismers hosted a small gathering at the cabin, sharing the season's work with their summer neighbours.

Near the end of Arthur's life, Long Beach became the couple's choice for their only annual retreat. Their last visit was in the summer of 1968; Arthur died the next year.

THE COMBERS RESORT AND LONG BEACH BUNGALOWS

The next people to fall in love with Long Beach enough to move there permanently and start a resort were Edgar and Evelyn Buckle and their boys, Neil and Dennis. It was a homecoming of sorts, as Evelyn had visited the beach as a child when her father, Frank Garrard, worked on the coast as a lineman. It took only two visits in 1949 to convince her husband and sons that relocating from Victoria made sense.

Neil Buckle was only twelve when they first arrived in Ucluelet on the *Uchuck*. A westerly was blowing spindrifts and little bits of paper, rubble, and dust down the gravel road to the dock. Someone was shooting at the crows above the local store. "I could hear the bullet zinging off into the bush," he later recalled, adding he felt he'd stepped into a Western movie. Any qualms he had, though, rolled away like the fog bank that lifted as the family drove over a hill and dropped down to Long Beach. After helping to unload, the boys were let loose on the beach. "We walked from one end of the beach to the other time and time again," said Neil. "I just fell in love with the place."

The rest of the family felt the same way, and by Christmas 1950 they were packing up the last of their boxes and getting ready to make the big trek to their new home near Sandhill Creek and a section of Long Beach locally called Combers.

The Buckles' plan was to set up a resort similar to the Donahues' Camp Maquinna, with a few simple cabins. At first, the family lived in a tent and a house that belonged to a previous Long Beach settler while they began pushing in a road and clearing a lot for the house site. Edgar's early death from cancer in 1954 was a blow and stalled the family's plans, but Evelyn and the boys persevered and succeeded in completing the house and their resort, which eventually came to be known as The Combers Resort.

The third family to move up to the beach at the time and develop a resort were the Moraes: Jack, Norah, and their three teenage boys. They, like the Buckles, were from Victoria and had been looking for a change in place and routine. In 1953, they bought a quarter section with a long stretch of beachfront next to Wickaninnish Lodge. They named their business Long Beach Bungalows.

The Long Beach Community Expands

Through the 1950s, not only was the number of small resorts on Long Beach increasing, but so was the size of the community. The Lovekins still had their house on the hill, now being enjoyed by the family's second and third generations. Many other cabins and permanent homes had been built in the area by then, both along the Ucluelet-Tofino road and on the beach. A few Tla-o-qui-aht families lived permanently at Esowista, and at Schooner Cove were several cabins, including one owned by the Hillier family, passed down from the days when the Hillier brothers helped George Jackson clear land for his "Hesawista" subdivision.

In 1958, Tofino resident George Nicholson summarized the picture at Long Beach this way: "The present settlement of this coming seaside resort comprises about 30 permanent homes, four resorts (with cabins), and 50 summer cottages occupied during the summer months by owners from different parts of the Island and the mainland. All the buildings are partly hidden, for the entire waterfront is still heavily wooded."

A Road Runs to It

The long-promised road to link the west coast to the rest of the island finally did become a reality. On August 24, 1959, the *Vancouver Sun* reported that a cavalcade of seventy-four cars loaded with three hundred ecstatic Tofino and Ucluelet residents arrived at Port Alberni, the first unofficial party to drive over the new gravel-and-dust route.

THE COLD WAR COMES TO LONG BEACH

One of Neil Buckle's first vivid memories of his life at Long Beach happened on the beach near his home at Sandhill Creek. It was 1953, and the air force had arrived to set up large cloth targets, each with a big bull's eye, on the beach. Sentries at both ends of the beach kept people out of the area because every morning at about 6 A.M. for six weeks, fighter planes zoomed in to strafe the beach and fire rockets at barrels anchored in the surf zone. While few residents and visitors could have been thrilled at the war-zone commotion tearing up their paradise, local teenage boys thought the display wildly exciting. Neil Buckle remembers clearly the scream of the shells followed by "thuds and sand flying everywhere" and "holes in the beach three feet deep." Razor clams in the intertidal zone took a particular beating, great numbers floating ashore in broken surrender.

World War II was over, but in the Western world, the Cold War was just beginning. Fears of a communist threat proliferated, the Korean War was underway, and anxieties abounded over North America's vulnerability to attack from nuclear weapons and long-range bombers. Although RCAF Base Tofino was closed, the large runways were still used for training flights, not to mention combat exercises like strafing Long Beach or using Florencia Island for target practice. (In the 1970s, three unexploded bombs were found on Florencia Island.)

To counter a potential attack from the Soviet Union, Canada and the United States developed an early warning system. The idea was to build a series of radar defences to detect any incoming threats approaching the Canada–U.S. border. This "Pinetree Line" included an installation near Long Beach, which meant reactivating RCAF Base Tofino. In 1952, construction of the radar station began atop a prominent hill overlooking the coastline and Long Beach. Pinetree Station #36 included a radar antenna (later upgraded to four domes), a generator, and a BC

Telephone office on top of Radar Hill. Buildings to house a transmitter and a receiver were located on either side of the hill. The station was partially operational by 1954 and in full swing by 1955.

Once again, a military presence on the west coast brought a lot of activity to the Long Beach area, but life at the base this time was very different. Only a few hundred personnel were posted there, and the base included married quarters and housing for families. Many civilians also worked on the base and at Radar Hill as telephone operators, stenographers, and maintenance men. The base soon became the social hub for the area, hosting many events and activities—often open to the local communities—from badminton, bingo, and square dancing to children's parties, a choral group, Saturday movie matinees, and performances by "local thespians." The RCAF baseball team often played against teams from local logging camps or the First Nation community of Opitsat, and they sponsored Airforce Day at the base with sports, races, and ice cream for the children.

As before, this flurry of activity at the base was intense but brief. The radar station closed in January 1958, its purpose redundant with advances made in radar technology. At that point, the federal Department of Transport took over the airport. Commercial flights began using the runways, as did recreational pilots. Long Beach's immediate usefulness to the military was once again over.

After that initial christening, Highway 4 was officially opened on September 4, 1959. "Highway" was perhaps overstating the nature of the thoroughfare, which as welcome as it was, in no way presumed to be a multi-lane graded and paved route. The highway linked two logging roads, one from the west coast and one from Sproat Lake, to a thirty-kilometre (eighteen-mile) stretch of government-built road in the middle. Narrow in parts, devoid of barriers, and often muddy and pothole-riddled, the route also included a series of steep switchbacks high above Sproat Lake that were especially terrifying to negotiate in the dark or fog. Because the roads were being used for active logging, gates on either end of the highway were closed to public traffic from 7 A.M. to 5 P.M. on weekdays. Just on weekends and holidays was access unrestricted. Not that the hazard of colliding with a fully loaded logging truck barrelling around a blind corner deterred everyone from making a dash for it on weekdays. Forestry crews kept a supply of padlocks handy to replace those hacked off the gates by people not keen on sticking with the new highway's rules.

RUDE AWAKENING

The early euphoria over improved accessibility soon gave way to alarm among residents about what the open door to their playground heralded. It was great that west coast residents had a road route out, but this also meant that outsiders had an easier route in. Hardly had the dust from that inaugural cavalcade settled than the new reality set in.

Upon seeing the beach, an inordinate number of car-owning visitors had no other thought but to drive out onto the glistening sand and use it as a natural speedway. This wasn't a new phenomenon, of course, as demonstrated by the first "motorized" visitors to Long Beach thirty years before, and, of course, locals had been using it as part of the Ucluelet-Tofino highway for years. Only now, many more people were showing up to blast across the beach and grind doughnuts in the sand, and the cars they drove were much faster and more destructive than old models. Wrote *Vancouver Sun* columnist Alan Fotheringham in a June 30, 1961, piece: "I drove the length of the beach, most of it at 70 mph... When the tide is out and the hard-packed sand stretches a half-mile, you can hit 100. No other beach this side of Daytona can make that statement."

Residents watched, both amused and appalled as tourists tore up and down the beach and through the surf, often becoming swamped at the mouth of Sandhill Creek or mired in the wet sand. Many cars were so hopelessly stuck or their transmissions seized up with salt water that the owners just left them. To this day, every once in a while, especially in winter when storms and high tides have scoured the beach, a corroded chassis emerges from the sand.

Meanwhile, longtime residents of the area struggled to adjust to the flood of newcomers wandering not just on the beach but on their properties. Hardly two months had passed after the road opened that the Lovekins, Peg Whittington, and other beach-front locals found themselves dealing with uninvited visitors knocking at the door looking for water, a toilet, a phone, or help to rescue a vehicle stuck in the sand. At wit's end, the Lovekins resorted to putting up a barbed-wire fence along the front of their property to preserve their privacy.

Despite the increased tourist traffic, residents consoled themselves with the fact that it was at least limited mainly to

For years, Long Beach was officially part of the highway system. High traffic, particularly on busy summer weekends, eventually led to the installation of traffic signs, including one setting the speed limit to twenty mph on the beach.

the summer and to certain sections of the beach. For most of the rest of the year, peace prevailed, and the beach had time to recover.

COMMUNITY IN TRANSITION

The community of Long Beach had also continued to grow over the years. By the early 1960s, at least sixty-three adult residents lived there full-time, with summer residents bumping that up to several hundred. The Moraes of Long Beach Bungalows had subdivided their property, and a collection of homes and businesses had been built near the beach and on the road down from the main highway. There was even a post office and a gas pump, and peacocks from Abbott's Store roamed freely about, as did children and dogs. There were more homes and businesses—a motel, gas station, store, and a few cafés—along the Tofino-Ucluelet highway and even a small school, Long Beach Elementary, located up toward Schooner Cove. A defunct hangar at the airport was home to the very active Long Beach Curling Club. Residents from Tofino, Ucluelet, and Long Beach chipped in $700 to buy it, and volunteers prepared and maintained the ice each season.

Among the original resort owners at Long Beach, faces and operations were changing, too. The Donahues had left the beach and Camp Maquinna, and another couple, Esther and Terry Wilson, stepped in as caretakers of the Lovekin property. Neil Buckle and his wife, Marilyn, took over the cabins Neil's family had built at The Combers Resort and added several more. The Moraes sold the Long Beach Bungalows to Doreen and Grant Myers. Only Peg Whittington and Singing Sands carried on as before, popular as ever with summer guests, most being longtime regulars. The biggest change in Long Beach's small tourism sector was the new developments of Wickaninnish Lodge.

The Wickaninnish Inn

As soon as Robin Fells saw the west coast for the first time, he knew he wanted to live there. The Vancouver account executive struck up a friendship, and later a business deal, with Joe Webb. Joe had a vision of expanding his resort, seeing in its place a larger, more upscale facility, but still preserving the relaxed atmosphere of Wickaninnish Lodge. Fells crafted this vision and a business plan that he carried from bank to investor in an attempt to secure funding. Vancouver businessman Jeff Crawford eventually stepped in as a partner, providing $50,000 in financing

The Wickaninnish Inn at Long Beach offered surf casting, clamming, beach-combing, and dancing ("whenever desired"). Its dress code: always informal.

so the project could move forward. In July 1964, the first guests were being welcomed at the twenty-two-room Wickaninnish Inn, whose restaurant and bar capitalized fully on the property's most spectacular asset: a panoramic view of the Pacific. The brochures announced, "No radio, No newspapers, No television, No telephones." Though informality was the inn's byword, its wall-to-wall carpeted rooms were well equipped and full-service dining facilities fairly chi-chi for the era and location.

Juxtaposed at the opposite end of Long Beach's accommodation options was its first campground: eighty-nine sites opened at Wickaninnish Provincial Park, which had been established at Green Point in 1962. Camping anywhere along the beach was also catching on, of course, amenities or not. After all, there was nothing like it anywhere in British Columbia. Where else could a family or group of friends pitch a tent or pull their camper right onto a west coast beach?

Waikiki North

"Do you know that these West Coast beaches are better than those of the south of France? They are wider, longer and more spacious, generally with colorful surroundings, and the sand is clean and silvery. The breakers can be 'shot' or 'ridden' just as effectively as those of Waikiki and Australia."

So wrote west coast resident R. Bruce Scott in 1937 (who must have considered the numbing water temperature too minor to mention). As prophetic as he was, even Scott wasn't the first to mention the possibility of this new water sport for Long Beach. As early as 1929, Gertrude Jackson wrote about the potential for "surf board riding" in a long plea for a road to the west coast. However, it took until the mid-1960s for words to translate into boards on the beach. Once people started tackling Highway 4, word quickly trickled out about the "new gold" to be mined at Long Beach and Wreck Bay: surf, beach camping, and breathtaking beauty—all in infinite supply and all free for the taking. The bonanza began.

The earliest of the area's surfers came from elsewhere on Vancouver Island and from the Lower Mainland. They had picked up the sport in California, Hawaii, and even at other breaks down the coast of Vancouver Island. Soon, a few surfers moved to area where they could indulge in their obsession as close to full time as possible. The surfing buzz was soon out, recalls Bruce Atkey, one of the first members of Long Beach's surf community. "Here was a place you could surf, camp, and lie naked on the beach." Atkey often had the waves all to himself, and if he did have company,

Early to surfing at Long Beach, Jim Sadler was known for his innovative oven-mitt-like hand paddles and his fearless pursuit of big waves. Here, Sadler rides his homemade board in Long Beach's first surf competition held in 1966.

it was likely Jim Sadler, another surfing original. Atkey had got his start surfing at Jordan River near Sooke, and Sadler at Pachena Bay near Bamfield. It wasn't long before a few other locals caught the surfing bug, too, including some of the crew building the new Wickaninnish Inn. Suddenly, there were days where surf conditions dictated the project's construction schedule.

All the early surfers were committed and passionate self-starters who had to make do with limited gear. No local surf shops at the time meant surfers had to travel to California for their gear or get creative with what was on hand. Wet suits were often ill-fitting dive suits, and many first boards were built from plans found in *Popular Mechanics*. The region's first surf competitions took place then, too, with the earliest being held at Long

Beach in 1966. Along with prizes for the best ride, there were also more unusual categories such as the best surfing scar. It was a modest beginning for an area that is today chock-a-block with surf shops and surf schools and that stages competitions attended by the world's top surfers.

The allure of the big breakers and wide open spaces that had started drawing surfers to the west coast was captivating another group, too, though their interest had little to do with sport.

Turned On and Tuned In:
The Flower Children Find Wreck Bay

July 20, 1969. Around the world, more than 500 million people were watching as moon-mission astronaut Neil Armstrong announced to the world, "The *Eagle* has landed." Six and a half hours later, he stepped onto the moon's surface.

Down at Wreck Bay, dozens of people sat at the mouth of Lost Shoe Creek, clustered around Godfrey Stephens' short-wave radio to listen to the historic event. Fires dotted the beach, the air pulsed with drumbeats, and the smell of wood smoke and dope filled the night air. Peyote buds had been tossed around like candy at a parade during the day, and the beach was primed for a party. Somewhere between two hundred and three hundred people were living at Wreck Bay that summer, and a momentous space trip to this tribe was clearly something to be celebrated in kind.

In the late 1960s, Wreck Bay was a west coast mecca for a new wave of settler looking for a better way of life. It was an era of social and political upheaval. The war in Vietnam raged. The threat of nuclear Armageddon loomed. And movements like women's liberation and Black Power were changing the everyday life across Western society. In a world that seemed in such

At Florencia (Wreck) Bay, Schooner Cove, Radar Beach, and elsewhere in the Long Beach area, people showed great imagination coupled with ingenuity to build their homes. They used driftwood boards, beach logs, beachcombed chains, and other pieces salvaged from the shore, forest, or dump to improvise dwellings.

turmoil, escape to Wreck Bay seemed a good solution, so that's what many people, mostly youth, did. Hippies, "flower children," bohemians, Vietnam war resistors and young vets, draft dodgers, beatniks riding that waning wave all arrived at Wreck Bay like summoned exiles. They shed past identities, last names, and often their clothes. They built shelters in the beach logs, putting up a tent or just a piece of plastic. Some stayed in clusters, others spread out down the five-kilometre (three-mile) beach to find seclusion. Meals were often communal, a sharing of whatever could be cobbled together—like mussels, crabs, fish, and berries, supplemented with rice or oats—though hitchhiking into Ucluelet for a beer and a burger wasn't out of the question. They played drums and flutes, carved sculptures from driftwood, cast candles in the sand, created poems from the ether, moulded pots from the clay of the Wreck Bay cliffs. A joint, a jug of cheap wine, or a tab of acid was rarely far out of reach.

Many of the beach dwellers developed a craft or art to help them generate a bit of cash. In that, Godfrey Stephens and many of his neighbours at the bay had a valuable ally in Norma Baillie, a woman who, before the most recent wave of Wreck Bay "settlers," had lived there with her children for many summers in an old miner's cabin. In 1967, she moved to Ucluelet full-time and opened a gift shop and gallery she named "The Wreckage," which was built for her by Bruce Atkey. Norma often bought the work of Stephens and others, taking their carvings, patchwork clothing, candles, crochet and macramé work, and wall hangings and mobiles made with stone, bone, feathers, and shell. She became not only a pay cheque for many of the young people, but also a confidante, advisor, counsellor, and friend. "Norma would be very motherly to us," remembers John Genn, who spent a few of those summers at Wreck Bay, "because we were irresponsible hippies. She'd say 'I'll give you $80 for the carving, but I'm only going to give it to you $20 a time.' She didn't want us to blow it all at once."

For the most part, tensions were few between the hippies and other residents. Long Beach residents regularly gave lifts to Wreck Bay hitchhikers (including, a few times, the young Margaret Sinclair before she went on to become Prime Minister Pierre Trudeau's wife), and there was, overall, tolerance for different ways of living. Still, flare-ups happened. On one occasion, a local bunch of vigilantes took offence to some hippies squatting in the sand dunes at Long Beach and marched down there threatening to cut their hair. Other residents and business owners were concerned that the hippies were taking over the beaches like they owned them and that their presence—especially when their presence appeared in the nude—might deter "legitimate tourists." Dave Hardy, a reporter for the *Vancouver Sun,* characterized the testiness as a "conflict between nature in the raw and people in the raw."

It was easy to love Wreck Bay on a sunny summer day. During the peak years of its time as a peace-and-love haven, up to five hundred people are thought to have been living on the beach at some points in the summer. When fall and winter rolled in, the numbers always dwindled, usually to fewer than thirty. Many of the "summer hippies" drifted away to warmer and drier climates when the weather turned poor or they had school, jobs, and families in the city to get back to. The die-hards who stuck it out year-round were those who fully embraced the idea of living "off the grid." Two of those were Merlin and Linda Bradley, who had built a substantial home near Lost Shoe Creek. They were one of the few Wreck Bay residents with a young family. Three other full-timers are almost always remembered as a trio: Chris Banke, Paul Jeffries, and Tom Richardson. They, too, built more substantial dwellings than their itinerant summertime neighbours, well away from the high tides and huge seas of winter. To survive, they sold their carvings and art and also picked up short-term jobs like working on boats during the fishing season.

More than forty years later, people who experienced those heady days at Wreck Bay talk of them mostly with fondness, as a time when they and hundreds of others were swept up in a grand experiment, trying to find a new way to live in a world that seemed hopelessly fractured and dysfunctional. "It was the

PEG'S KIDS

During the 1960s and into the early 1970s, Peg Whittington's cabins and property became a *de facto* home for many young people who found themselves carried in with the era's tide to Long Beach. While she catered to her usual visitors in the tourist season, in the winter months she rented the cabins on a long-term basis to the many "kids" she befriended.

It was art that seemed to be a draw for many of the young people who lived at Peg's, like Darlene Choquette, whom Peg once referred to as "my first hippie." Peg had high regard for the creative life and, says Choquette, she "really thought you needed to express yourself in some way." Artists of all disciplines, some highly trained, many self-taught or just experimenting, gathered at her cabins. Many went on to become part of the fabric of Canadian arts, including poets Susan Musgrave and Sean Virgo, musicians Valdy and Kent Fiddy, and actress Frances Hyland. Playwright George Ryga was also a frequent guest with his wife, Norma. In fact, when the National Arts Centre in Ottawa chose Ryga's highly acclaimed play *The Ecstasy of Rita Joe* to open its new studio theatre in 1969, a local newspaper reported that "everybody who was anybody was in the house to share the champagne. Everybody that is, except playwright George Ryga who was ... at Singing Sands."

Many people loved Peg and became close to her, said her longtime friend Jim Darling. "She encompassed the entire spirit of [Long Beach]. She was key to many things. It all radiated from her."

healing of the place that really attracted us," one former beach dweller recalls of the time. "There was lots of change in the world and lots of experimentation, but the beach rejuvenated us."

Mayhem at the Tide Pool

"Six near-drownings, a water-damaged late model car, beach sand sleighing... have all contributed to an extremely busy full past week," reads a report by one of the provincial park's summer naturalists in 1968. The undertow on the rocks off Green Point (where Dick Whittington died in 1946) had almost caused the drowning, and the car in question had sunk so quickly that the water was up to the dashboard before the driver and his two young children could escape. The "sand sleighing" mentioned by the naturalist referred to an activity where a rider clung to a log or upturned car hood tied by a rope to a car driven at high speed down the beach. "Occasionally driftlogs or slight depressions in the sand send the rider sprawling," the report continued. Sand sleighing later evolved into "pallet surfing," with cars now towing riders who stood or kneeled on a wooden pallet and "surfed," again at breakneck speed. Weaving in and out of the many pilings that still stood in the sand after World War II only added to the thrill. If a hard fall didn't injure you, being struck by oncoming car traffic on the beach might. Just two years before, an eighteen-year-old Vancouver boy was hit by a car and killed while strolling the beach.

Long Beach and Wreck Bay had become the focus of a growing but bittersweet love affair between the environment and the public. Here, however, was a textbook example of a system cycling wildly out of balance. The passions and pressures were mounting, and before long something was going to give.

9

in the park's
embrace

THE HIGH rounded pile taking shape before us is like a Provençal haystack in a Van Gogh painting. Only we're not in France, and it's not a stack of hay. We're at the top of Radar Hill, and the stack is Scotch broom. I'm part of a team of about a dozen volunteers who have come for a "broom bash," an attempt to eradicate a foreign invader, from this hilltop at least. During the Cold War, while radar technicians and other military personnel were preoccupied monitoring the skies and seas for any suspicious activity, right under their noses another foreign menace was sinking its roots into the soil around the radar station.

The vibrant yellow peavine-like flowers of the Scotch broom are a familiar sight to anyone travelling on southern Vancouver

Island. Every spring, the bright, cheery-looking bushes, typically one to three metres (three to ten feet) tall, splash colour along rural roadsides, logging cutblocks, uncultivated fields, ditches, and vacant city lots. It took just three seeds of this perennial shrub, germinated in the soils of Sooke in 1850, to start a botanical conflagration. Captain Walter Colquhoun Grant, an immigrant from Scotland perhaps pining for the yellow hills of home, brought the broom to Vancouver Island, and they've been flinging their seeds with vigorous abandon ever since. On hot dry days, the plant's slender black pods snap open, catapulting the seeds in every direction. Even one new seedling establishing on a patch of soil can make a big impact. A mature shrub can produce 15,000 seeds annually, any of which can remain viable in the soil for up to 30 years, ready to sprout when conditions are right. And on Vancouver Island, that's often. For more than 150 years, the plant has been slowly and insidiously taking over native habitat, crowding and choking out indigenous plants.

In total, the results of our assault filled five large dump trucks with broom that day, and only constant vigilance by retired park naturalist Barry Campbell in the years since has kept the scourge under control. Still, it's a war that's far from over. Even after our intensive efforts on the site, Campbell has pulled another 96,000 seedlings from there as of summer 2011.

When does an introduced plant species become a pest? For ecologists, it's when the species out-competes native plants for habitat, hogging water, food, land, or all three, often reproducing unchecked in the absence of natural controls. Changing the environment in a way that alters native plants and topographies is another sign that a new species can become a problem—for example, the way that European beach grass has afflicted Long Beach's sand dunes. Not all introduced species bother us. If they're edible, like Japanese oysters and clams, or beautiful, like the flowers that fill our gardens, we may welcome them. It is all a matter of perspective.

Humans at Long Beach are arguably as much of an introduced species as Scotch broom and European beach grass in the Long Beach area. Their impact on the west coast's natural environment, from its ocean waters, tidal zones, and rivers to its mudflats, beaches, bogs, and forests, has varied widely over the millennia. We may therefore ask ourselves: Are we invasive or beneficial? Part of the problem or just part of a continuum of change?

The Park Idea: Slow Speed Ahead

Word of Long Beach being made into a national park had been circulating widely in the late 1960s, but it certainly wasn't the first time the idea had been floated. The Canadian National Parks Association had made a resolution supporting the idea of a Long Beach national park in 1929. Two years later, in February 1931, Gertrude Jackson had three visitors drop in and sign her guest book: F.D. Mulholland, chief, Surveys Division for the BC Forest Service; H.T. Garden, B.C. land surveyor; and J.M. Wardle, chief engineer for the National Parks of Canada. The men spent several days touring the Long Beach area to assess its worthiness for national park status.

In his follow-up report, Wardle described the beach at Long Bay as one of the finest he had seen ("compares very favourably with some of the better known beaches... of Oregon and California"), but his list of drawbacks outweighed the pluses: no suitable location for a wharf on the Long Bay side (thus precluding boating)... water too cold for bathing... summer fogs that didn't dissipate until noon... the prevailing westerly wind... a dangerous undertow.

Even if the chief engineer for national parks wasn't keen on a Long Beach national park, plenty of local boosters were, lobbying even back then for a park to protect the land for the public. Some efforts were made in that direction by the provincial government (setting Green Point aside, for example, in 1948), but the majority of people saw little need to protect the area for the public when relatively few actually visited. Not until the mounting bedlam on the beach became impossible to ignore in the 1960s did the need to protect the land *from* the public gain serious attention. Establishment of Wickaninnish Provincial Park in 1962 at Long Beach, with its campground at Green Point and a few beachfront sections, was a start.

Calls for a national park continued, however, with local communities making the loudest noise. Arthur Laing, the federal minister responsible for parks at the time, let it be known he thought Mount Garibaldi north of Vancouver might be a great location for a new national park in British Columbia. Tofino's Tom Gibson and others representing west coast businesses registered their vehement disagreement, saying there were more than enough mountain parks in the province but no national parks that preserved and celebrated the ocean and seashore. Given all they had had to endure in the post-road years, beach residents were also asking for a park just to protect the beach from, as Peg Whittington put it, "hoodlums and rough people and racing on the beach." Plus, she added, "We needed toilets. The beach stunk."

By September 1966, it seemed as if the provincial and federal governments were close to a deal, sweetened when the province offered Wickaninnish Provincial Park as the nucleus of a larger coastal national park. Minister Laing told the provincial recreation minister, Ken Kiernan, he would "act with the speed of light" to move the deal forward.

On busy summer weekends, cars and campers often covered Long Beach, especially near beach access points. This photo was taken during the Long Beach Fly In. During the annual spring event, flying clubs descended on the airport, and sometimes the beach. The Long Beach Curling Club coordinated the entertainment with a fundraising crab feast and dance.

The initial idea was to expand the existing provincial park, adding the coastline from Schooner Cove to Cox Bay, but the federal government felt this was too small an area for a national park. It therefore sent a team to British Columbia in the spring of 1967 to look for other options. In Tofino, the team was sought out by one of the most enthusiastic boosters of a national park, Howard McDiarmid, a local doctor. McDiarmid was also a rookie MLA in the Social Credit Party, having won the Alberni constituency the previous fall. A key part of McDiarmid's electoral platform had been to secure national park status for Long Beach, and when he won his seat in the provincial legislature he wasted no time moving on the cause.

Lifestyle preferences, age, and general world outlook tended to separate where people lived and vacationed in the Long Beach area. Florencia (Wreck) Bay and more secluded beaches at Radar Beach or Schooner Cove were the main draw for youth and those with "alternative" ideas.

In one of his more memorable speeches, delivered at the provincial legislature in February 1968, McDiarmid decried the lack of control provincial park officials had over the activities taking place on Long Beach, and he reiterated his position that a national park was the only way to rein in the chaos of cars, planes, and campers threatening to ruin the area.

"Are you aware, Mr. Speaker," McDiarmid began, "that on July 1 of last year there were 7,000 campers tenting on Long Beach provincial park, crammed in cheek by jowl, defecating, micturating and copulating—not separated by so much as a blade of grass, Mr. Speaker? In fact, barely a grain of sand. Motorcycles racing up and down the beach, airplanes landing and taking off, no water and two toilets for 7,000 people?"

His message, as he'd intended, received extensive media attention. (McDiarmid later wrote in his memoirs that he'd resorted to using medical terminology in that speech so the Speaker of the House wouldn't rule him out of order for using the "common descriptions" of the activities he was describing.) McDiarmid also deplored the inability of the government to do much about the squatters. On another occasion, he held up an article from the *Vancouver Sun* that showed a man and woman, both naked, walking hand in hand on the beach. "Public nudity occurs particularly on the beach known locally as Wreck Bay... and while I understand that this form of rapport with nature is fairly widespread... in the Scandinavian countries, Wreck Bay is neither Sweden nor the Garden of Eden. I think it is a fair statement to say that most Canadians are rather embarrassed and intimidated by this form of behaviour."

While the idea of a national park on the west coast was now firmly in the minds of British Columbia citizens and their politicians, the negotiations between the two levels of government dragged, lumbered down by disagreement over who would pay for land acquisition. "About that speed of light" a *Vancouver Sun* editorial read on March 1, 1968, calling Laing on his promise for a fast resolution on a park and asking why British Columbians should put up with "slum conditions on their sole major ocean beach for still another year."

The turning point came in the summer of 1968, when Jean Chrétien replaced Laing as minister of Indian Affairs and Northern Development, with responsibility for national parks. The province was keen to have Chrétien visit the coast to see it first-hand, and provincial minister Kiernan extended an invitation. Chrétien accepted, and the visit was set for November 25, 1968.

Closing the Deal

At Long Beach and in the local communities, the real possibility of a national park was positive news to most. With a park would come the necessary infrastructure to support thousands of visitors, as well as rules over what was acceptable behavior in the area and what was not. And most residents living at and near the beach believed that for them the status quo would be maintained. National parks in the Rocky Mountains—Banff and Jasper—had set a precedent for the inclusion of town sites, cottages, and businesses within the park boundary. Surely that would be the case here.

Chrétien arrived amid much excitement and great expectations. After being toured up the coast by helicopter to view the other sections being considered for the park, his party was set down at Long Beach. The local chambers of commerce had organized a luncheon at the Wickaninnish Inn, a spot that would give the federal minister a front-row seat overlooking the beach while he enjoyed his clam chowder.

Following a meeting between Chrétien and Kiernan the next day, the west coast was a solid handshake closer to its first big park. In March 1969, the British Columbia legislature passed the West Coast National Parks Act, which provided the legal vehicle for creating a park with three units. Long Beach would be developed first, with the units in Barkley Sound and between Cape Beale and Port Renfrew (the West Coast Trail) following later. The two levels of government had agreed to split the cost of acquiring land.

It took another year before the deal was sealed with the federal partner. In April 1970, Kiernan and Chrétien signed the agreement formalizing the park's creation. The park boundaries extended from Wya Point south of Florencia Bay to the south end of Cox Bay and across Esowista Peninsula to Grice Bay. The new park protected the land from further development and also installed a new landlord—the federal government—which could provide staff and some capital to deal with the pressing issues of overcrowding and lack of facilities.

At Long Beach, the announcement made little difference to day-to-day life. All of the work at this stage was in the hands of bureaucrats, hammering out the minutiae and legal details about boundaries, land acquisitions, and payment sharing. On the beach, it was pretty much business as usual. Resorts were booked solid during the tourist season, and the campground overflowed onto the beach. Weekends, particularly long weekends, stretched the skeleton provincial park staff. Adding to the stress of having to deal with too many people and cars was the growing concern over what was happening to the area's natural resources. The extent of razor clam harvesting had long been cause for alarm. As one employee reported, "Clammers equipped with clam guns and shovels flock onto the lower beach during low tides and indiscriminately gather hundreds of pounds of razor clams. Many times this summer I caught people with two or three large garbage cans full of clams."

Another issue was the collecting of sea stars. "It seems campers needed a starfish to prove they had visited British Columbia's West Coast," wrote one park employee, adding that many of the marine animals were then simply abandoned after someone had dried, or attempted to dry, them in the sun. "The maintenance staff tell me they have found as many as fifty dead starfishes in garbage cans in one day."

Peg Whittington had watched many changes over her thirty years at Long Beach, but nothing like this distressing state of affairs: the vehicles, the parties, the amount of garbage, the mindless destruction. She was supportive of the infrastructure and control a national park might offer even as she realized that such a change might come at a personal cost to her. (As an example of her generosity, she worked closely with park staff, allowing naturalists to hold early evening talks at her resort. Some of the early park staff lived in her cabins.) The Lovekin family and other longtime residents shared Peg's sentiments and recognized the dilemma. As Steve Lovekin, grandson of A.C. and Helen, summed it up, "We could see that land was either going to be sold off to developers, with hotels soon lining the beach, or it was going to be park." In the end, however, protection of their beloved beach trumped the alternatives.

Saying Goodbye

At last, Long Beach was in the embrace of national park protection where it would be, in keeping with Canada's National Park Act, "maintained and made use of so as to leave [it] unimpaired for the enjoyment of future generations." But what of the present generation that now found itself living within a national park?

The answer to that question had in fact been revealed shortly before the formal announcement in April 1970. In a presentation in Ucluelet about the new park that January, William McKim, regional director of the National and Historic Parks Branch, made it clear that they would be assembling land "free of encumbrances," meaning that most of the residents currently living in the park were expected to be out ("relocated") by 1972.

"This news just came out of the blue," recalls Neil Buckle, owner of The Combers Resort. He, like many of the residents and business owners, had assumed they would be grandfathered in or that the resorts, cottages, and even the small community of Long Beach would be permitted to co-exist within park

STARS IN THE SEA

"But is it alive?" is a common question people ask when first seeing an ochre star, the most common type of sea star visible on the rocks near Long Beach. At low tide, clinging immobile to the algae-slick rocks often in a jumbled pile, they do look dead. But when the tide comes in, sea stars get busy. Time-lapse photography shows them roaming the intertidal zone, moving up with the rising tide and then back down again as the water recedes.

These animals typically prey on barnacles, chitons, and mussels, but theirs is an unusual hunt-and-dine *modus operandi.* Nudged up to a barnacle or chiton, the sea star everts its stomach out its mouth and prods the prey's soft tissues, which it then starts digesting. With a mussel, the sea star grasps the shell using its hundreds of tube feet tipped with tiny suction cups and pries the shell open ever so slightly in order to slip its stomach inside. The hinge of a mussel shell is strong, but not strong enough to endure the hydraulic system that powers sea star tube feet.

Early park naturalists at Long Beach had good reason to be concerned about the bags of sea stars being plucked off the rocks and left to die in plastic pails or garbage cans. Shore stars are key predators in the intertidal zone; their presence, or absence, greatly affects what other species move in or move out. In experiments involving the removal of sea stars from a section of seashore, mussel colonies migrated down the rocks more than a metre. Without their primary predator, the mussel population quickly started becoming a monoculture, on the road to out-competing and dominating that neighbourhood of the intertidal zone.

boundaries. However, the philosophy of national parks had shifted since the days when those in Banff and Jasper had been formed in the early 1900s. In the 1970s, the view was that national parks should be maintained as wilderness areas, as free of development as possible.

The idea of a wilderness park free of encumbrances and permanent residents also extended to First Nations, at least at first. When park boundaries and lands were being determined, the fate of the reserves that fell within those boundaries was on government minds. They considered different arrangements, including purchasing the lands or swapping them for similar-sized parcels elsewhere. For the most part, this came as a surprise to the area's First Nations, who once again saw a government discussing the future of their lands without meaningful consultation. In the end, the reserve lands were not expropriated.

CLEARING OUT LONG BEACH

By the time Prime Minister Pierre Trudeau helicoptered into Long Beach for a visit on June 16, 1970, residents and businesses within the boundary of the park had received the expected letter: "A perusal of the map indicates that your property comes within the National Park boundary and consequently Bill 73 [the West Coast National Parks Act], which is attached, now takes effect." Lands, stated the act, could be acquired by "purchase, gift, exchange or expropriation."

Surveyors arrived to measure out the lots in private hands on behalf of the government, and some landowners had their own surveys done as well. Then the negotiations began. The task of assembling the land fell to provincial authorities, in this case the Department of Highways and Department of Recreation and Conservation, Parks Branch. For some property owners,

Despite having received letters from the government notifying them they had to leave their Long Beach homes, residents graciously welcomed Prime Minister Pierre Trudeau on his visit in 1970.

being booted out of the coming park was great news. Those who rarely if ever visited their property were happy for the effortless cash. For other owners, it was a devastating prospect and meant walking away from a lifetime home, a retirement dream, or an established family business.

Settlements varied from property to property. Often, the final figure depended on the landowner's willingness to spend time and money preparing counter-offers. In one case, an owner

While visiting Long Beach, Prime Minister Pierre Trudeau tried surfing for the first time. He borrowed a wetsuit and a board from Robin Fells and staff at the Wickaninnish Inn and, true to form, stood up on his first attempt.

was offered $11,354 per acre, a figure arrived at by averaging the sale of the two lots of comparable land on either side: the owner on the left had received $7,778 per acre, whereas the owner on the right had received $14,930 per acre. Several landowners scored a coup when they discovered they actually owned more land than they had originally acquired. The lot that had once been in Ada Leverson's name (bought for her by her husband in 1908) was a case in point. By 1971, when the land acquisition deals were underway, it was owned by Monashee Enterprises. The surveyors found the lot had grown by 2.37 hectares (5.87 acres) thanks to decades' worth of accretion of sand on the beachfront. Monashee had the time and finances to fight to be paid for the bonus area, and the Supreme Court ruled in its favour on that one.

Robin Fells at Wickaninnish Inn was determined not to give up his land without a fight, and he had many supporters to back him up. As soon as word got out that the inn might be closed, the letter writing by past clientele began, urging the government to allow the inn to remain open. For Fells, as for many others faced with losing their businesses, it wasn't so much the money as the loss of a way of life. In the end, however, Fells had to give in, saying, "They'll say they didn't expropriate me, but what choice did I have?" He and his business partner were eventually bought out, but they also received a concession. The government, bowing to public pressure, agreed to lease the entire inn back to Fells for a five-year term. The arrangement was problematic, at least as far as Fells was concerned, and he left after a year, frustrated by an overly bureaucratic landlord who, among other things, wrote a formal letter chastising Fells for being out one penny in his lease payment calculation.

Fells's former employee John Allan and two partners took over running the business. When the lease again came up in 1977, the government seemed determined to end commercial enterprise in the park. Controversy over the state of the inn had been brewing for a while. Supporters argued that it was an asset to the area, a much-needed amenity and a stellar experience. But others insisted that the quality of the inn had slid drastically, and it was little more than a party palace for its staff, with a few customers along to foot the bill. The truth likely fell somewhere in between. In the end, Bill Billings—the last stalwart miner of Wreck Bay—was the final resident of the Wickaninnish Inn. After having to leave Wreck Bay, where he had lived in a cabin and doggedly sifted the sands for gold since the 1940s, he was living in a converted bread truck, but park officials asked him to caretake the inn buildings when it closed. Later, he would be allowed to live in a small cabin along the Long Beach Road. "The park let me down in a lot of ways," recalled Robin Fells, "but they let Billings stay in a house for the rest of his life; that was a good thing."

By the fall of 1977, the inn was closed. Parks Canada eventually converted the building into an interpretive centre and restaurant.

CLEARING OUT WRECK BAY

At Wreck Bay, the park designation had little effect at first. Most of the beach dwellers knew they would eventually be kicked out, but no great effort had yet been launched to do that. On the plus side, the park's new status meant the beach was somewhat cleaner. Surfer Bruce Atkey had won a contract to provide garbage removal services at Wreck Bay and also to build some outhouses.

It was what one *Vancouver Sun* reporter called a meeting between "the squatters and the squares." In May 1971, park superintendent George Trachuk asked the people living at Wreck Bay and other beaches to gather at the platform that had been erected at Green Point for the official park opening. Speaking from the plywood deck, he laid out the plan for the park and told the squatters that they needed to vacate their dwellings by September 30. He added that they'd be welcome to stay at the new beachfront campsite planned for Schooner Cove for $1.50 a night. To

When Princess Anne officially opened the new park on May 4, 1971, longtime Wreck Bay dweller Godfrey Stephens presented her with a wood sculpture that park officials had commissioned him to carve for the occasion. His fee: enough to cover the cost of a Klepper folding kayak. This photo shows the princess with Jean Chrétien, standing behind.

people able to live on $1.50 a *week* and quite content where they were, Trachuk's invitation fell flat. As for their beach and forest homes, Trachuk went on, all would be torn down. The squatters argued back—and even offered Trachuk a swig from a jug of red wine—saying that they were not hurting anyone and that their beach was more environmentally sound than Long Beach, where trucks, campers, and cars rode roughshod over the place. It was to no avail. The government's decision would not be subverted.

And indeed by the late fall of 1971, most of the shelters from Wreck Bay were gone. Anyone with a place had been offered $20 to $50 to destroy the structure and clean up the area before leaving.

Merlin and Linda Bradley were one couple evicted from Wreck Bay. Five weeks after the meeting at Green Point, Linda gave birth to a son, Aaron, in the family's cabin. In honour of the birth, this abstract pole, carved by Paul Jeffries, Daniel Lowry, Merlin Bradley, and Tom Richardson, was raised. It remained at Wreck Bay for several decades until winter storms washed it away in the early 2000s.

Many complied; others just walked away. A few resisted to the bitter end only to watch as park staff cleared the remaining shacks of their possessions before burning the structures down.

Growing Pains

The squatters were ousted, and land acquisition continued, but the situation in the park would get worse before it got better.

The early campground consisted of sites between the beach logs. On busy summer weekends, the beach was rimmed with cars, campers, and small tents. At times, cars and trucks became mired in the sand. Ruined vehicles were occasionally set on fire in a "car-be-que."

Park staff may have had some ability to impose controls on their visitors' activities now, but their efforts to do so—erecting speed signs on the beach, for example—were hard to impose and regulate on a beach that had been pretty much rule-free.

In the fall of 1972, paving work on the road linking the west coast and Port Alberni was completed. The project had also removed the switchbacks from the route. The way was now open for virtually any vehicle, high slung or low slung, to make the trip out to the new park.

West coast residents may have cheered the improvement, but what it held in store for their park was bluntly revealed on Easter weekend the next spring. Park staff counted seventeen hundred camping parties. About a thousand of those were on Long Beach alone, where tents and campers packed in several rows deep in some stretches. Other campers set up at Schooner Cove and Wreck Bay. Summer hadn't even started, and the park was already bursting with people.

But those figures were paltry once the May long weekend stormed in. An estimated ten thousand people arrived on the coast. One group of over three hundred people got so out of hand—even setting a car on fire and rolling it down the beach—that the RCMP invoked the Riot Act to gain order. The party ended with eleven people arrested.

The park's plan to ban cars and camping on the beach altogether was more vital than ever. However, even the non-rowdy, non-partying crowd objected to this step. The idea that the bad behaviour of some should spoil the privileges of everyone angered many. Most irked were the locals and longtime visitors who had valued and respected open access to the huge beaches, the mudflats, and the adjacent forests to harvest clams or crabs,

SURF SCHOOL 101

One of the most popular swimming spots at Long Beach—the area in front of the Lovekins' property, near a rock now called Lovekin Rock—is also one of the most dangerous. A strong rip current running beside the rock has proved deadly for many swimmers caught in it.

In the 1960s and '70s, more people coming to Long Beach, combined with surfing's growing popularity, became a recipe for trouble on the water. The park eventually installed lifeguards, but most of them were pool lifeguards, who had no experience with surfing or ocean rescues and whose hours at the beach were limited.

Two local young men, Kent Fiddy and Steve Richey, became frustrated by the park authorities' seeming lack of concern over water safety, and in 1972 they applied for and received an Opportunities for Youth grant to set up the Water Safety and Surf Apparatus School. They reasoned that surfers were the best qualified to educate people about water safety at Long Beach, given their intimate understanding of the ocean's behaviour and conditions in the area. Fiddy and Richey ran their surf school as a mobile operation from their van, usually teaching at a surf break called Tiny's, between Incinerator Rock and Esowista. They'd pull up there in the van, unload boards, and stick a flag in the sand advertising lessons, which were offered free of charge. Attendees were instructed on water safety as well. The school ran for three years, teaching more than eight hundred people. In that time, Fiddy and Richey also assisted park staff with several rescues and lobbied steadily for adequate signage and education to alert the public to the area's water hazards. Their efforts eventually led to the creation of a park surf guard program that is still in operation today.

to hunt water fowl and deer, to collect mushrooms and berries, and even to cut firewood.

Talk of banning camping and driving on the beach also was the last in a long list of complaints against the area's new landlord. Not only had the park authorities removed all of the places to rent a bed and buy a meal, fuel, or a container of milk within park boundaries, but now it seemed the goal was to remove people, too. *Vancouver Sun* columnist Bob Hunter referred to it as a "plot to steal Long Beach from the camping public."

A Quiet Beach Again

Life was not easy for park staff in the early days, no matter how stunning their natural surroundings. They bore the brunt of local resentments as the changes occurred, even though many decisions came down from Ottawa or the regional office in Calgary with seemingly little understanding of, or willingness to accommodate, the situation on the ground.

Three items seemed symbolic of this. One was the razing of the Lovekin house. The Lovekin family suggested it would make the perfect life-saving station, given that most of the accidents in the park occurred in the waters out in front of the house. Whichever way the house might be put to use, locals saw it as a beautiful building that should be maintained for something. In fact, it had been left vacant for a long while and suffered damage from both vandalism and the damp climate. Another sore point was the loss of the cabin that Group of Seven artist Arthur Lismer had enjoyed for so many years. The third point perhaps hurt most. While many of the beach's homeowners accepted their requirement to leave the beach, most could not forgive a bureaucracy that would separate Peg Whittington from her beloved beach and home of more than thirty years. If any exception was to be made, they felt, it should be to let Peg stay until the end of her life. In the end, all three went: the Lovekin house, the Lismer cabin, and Peg.

Through it all, the park authority held its course with an eye on the ultimate goal: that the park should be free of development and returned to as natural a state as possible. Once lands and buildings were legally acquired, houses and business premises were sold off (many homes in Tofino and Ucluelet today were moved from the beach) or burned down. Some stayed, becoming staff housing and offices. Little evidence of the homes and businesses formerly within the park remain today; in their place are hiking trails, picnic areas, and parking lots for day-use access to the beach.

Park officials finally closed the beach to camping and driving on Labour Day weekend 1975. Despite wide awareness of the reasons, the move was still controversial. Too little in the way of visitor services existed in Tofino and Ucluelet to support those coming to the area, and with the beach closed off except for walk-in camping at Schooner Cove, some people wondered if the fun and the attraction was gone, too.

At one point, a federal politician got an earful from frustrated residents when he arrived to check on the status of the park. He listened, but also tried to reassure the public that it would take time for a natural park to be appreciated—perhaps even twenty years.

He was, it turns out, right.

conclusion
ebb tide

I T IS oddly fitting that the day of my first surf lesson I find a
banana slug climbing up the sleeve of my wetsuit. Two west
coast icons, surfing and slugs, combine to underscore this true
Long Beach moment—and to remind me not to leave my wetsuit
flung on the beach logs too close to the forest's edge.

My friend Carallyn has offered to give me a few tips, and I
couldn't ask for a better teacher. Carallyn was one of the first
serious female surfers on the coast, and she received her first lesson right here at Incinerator over thirty years ago.

After the slug is removed and delivered back to the forest
where it belongs, I wriggle into my suit, and the lesson begins.
We first determine whether I am a goofy foot (right foot forward)

ECOTOURISM'S EARLY DAYS

On a quiet morning on Combers Beach, distinctive honks and roars often drift in across the beach from Sea Lion Rocks. If the wind is right, a distinctive smell can drift in, too. Sea Lion Rocks is home for part of the year to both California sea lions and Steller (Northern) sea lions. Both species use the rocks as a rest haul-out and base for feeding. The marine mammals' breeding rookeries are located elsewhere in the Pacific, but pups have occasionally been seen on these rocks. California sea lions are identified by the large bump on their heads (called the sagittal crest) and by their bark. Steller sea lions, compared with their California cousins, are much larger. Males can weigh as much as one thousand kilograms (over two thousand pounds). It is the Steller that puts the "lion" in sea lion. Along with its lion-like roar, its bulging neck and chest together create a shape like a leonine mane, and when they get moving, harrumphing along on their four limbs at a remarkable speed, the resemblance to their terrestrial namesake is apparent.

The boat-based ecotourism industry in the Long Beach area owes its start to sea lions, not grey whales as one might think. In 1968, Tofino resident Ernie Bach was the first to take tourists out for marine mammal viewing, with sea lions as the stars of the show. Bach would anchor his boat in the lee of the rocks near Esowista and row ashore to pick up people to take out to Sea Lion Rocks. It turned into a popular business. When Bach stopped doing the tours, Jim and Carolyn Hudnall stepped in. The couple, who had first arrived on the coast in the mid-1960s, were running harbour tours in Tofino. They submitted a proposal to park authorities suggesting they take over the sea lions tours, and Sea Lion Cruises was born. Each day, the couple drove to Long Beach from Tofino and sold tickets from the beach logs. Eventually, their company expanded to include a fleet of canoes that they rented for use on Grice Bay.

or regular, and then Carallyn draws the outline of a surfboard on the sand and gives me the finer points of positioning, paddling, and "popping up" on the board. Then we head into the water.

It's after Labour Day in September, so we have little company in the waves. The breeze is warm and light, and the sky is the crisp, crystalline blue of glacial ice. For the next hour, I do my best to stand up on my board—and even experience the exhilaration of catching a wave perfectly (still lying prone, mind you)—but after being tossed off and thumped in the shore break enough, I decide that floating on the board in the gentle swell will be just fine for a while.

I paddle outside the shore break and sit up, straddling my board. The rhythmic swell is calming after the thrashing I've endured in the breaking waves. On my right is Lovekin Rock, or Gull Island as it was once called, or *chah.wa.nis* before that, when Tla-o-qui-aht people used to gather gull eggs there. If George Jackson was still at his "House on the Hill" he could pick me out from his front porch, a black spot bobbing on the waves. I can also see down the beach toward where Peg Whittington and her "kids" lived, and up to the village of Esowista, where today rows of colourful houses line the beach. I think of all the stories played out on this landscape before me: of Father Brabant and Bishop Seghers plodding by, of Pete Hillier and his brothers hiking up the beach to visit Jackson, of the first cars and motorcycles racing along the expanse of sand with joy and wild abandon. So many stories and so many dreams have been played out on these shores.

In August 1970, *Vancouver Sun* columnist Bob Hunter wrote, "There are two Long Beaches. First, the 'old' Long Beach of long, long ago, like last summer. Or, if anyone was talking about Long Beach last summer, the old Long Beach meant the one of the summer before."

Hunter's words capture the magic of Long Beach perfectly. As if in a slow dissolve from one scene to the next in a film, the area's settings and players have constantly changed, each writing their own script for those moments they hold the spotlight in the Long Beach story. Despite all of these comings and goings, the physical beach and its surroundings have retained their unwavering allure. Out here on this wild edge, where sand, sea, and sky merge, people have always found a lot of space for thinking, dreaming, recharging.

I wonder, however, what I would be writing about now if Long Beach had not become part of a national park. Those early years of the park's birth were terribly bumpy, but now, forty years on, few people would argue that this move to preservation wasn't for the best. One only needs to walk along a sandy beach in Hawaii, California, or even Tofino to see how, eventually, beautiful beaches inevitably become lined with homes and hotels.

No doubt, the federal government's strategy for creating the park would be much different if the park was being formed today. Philosophies and goals evolve just as society's expectations do. As a case in point, when the park boundaries were being determined back in the late 1960s, government officials asked First Nations if they would be willing to swap reserve lands from inside the park for land outside it. Officials didn't want any people inside the park, even if their ancestors had been a part of this place for millennia. First Nations negotiators turned down the proposal, and so their lands remained within the boundaries of the park. Recently, however, for the first time in Canadian national park history, land was removed from Pacific Rim and given back to a First Nation. The Tla-o-qui-aht are now expanding their Long Beach village of Esowista with the construction of *Ty Hitaniis,* "a place to gather whales."

In many ways, as well, Long Beach today is the wildest it has been in the last century or so. This, too, has a lot to do with changing philosophies and the passage of time. Wolf and cougar populations in the Long Beach area have rebounded, for example, with the end of bounties and a shift in attitudes about wildlife. (This is a far cry from the earliest days of the park, when wolves were so rarely seen that a wolf killed on the highway had to be identified by experts just to confirm it wasn't a dog.)

Although the beach and forest trails may be busy during the day, at night the gates are locked and wildlife has the run of the beach. Now, early morning beach walkers can glean the stories that have unfolded in the night by deciphering any animal tracks they find on the wet, bare sand.

With the next flood tide, these tracks will be washed away again, readying the beach for the coming chapters.

acknowledgements

THIS BOOK would have been much more difficult to write if it were not for the tireless efforts of Barry Campbell. Barry was one of Pacific Rim National Park Reserve's first naturalists, and his interest in history and his meticulous skills at preserving documents, photographs, maps, and more have been invaluable. Barry was supportive throughout the writing of this book and was patient with my many emails, phone calls, and visits to his kitchen. Our bush-bashes were such welcome trips away from my desk. He also graciously vetted many of the chapters in their draft form.

Thanks to my publishers, Rob Sanders and Nancy Flight, who saw promise in this idea and wisely nudged me in directions I was hesitant to go. Georgina Montgomery gently helped me put an unwieldy tome out of its misery. Her shaping and finessing of a manuscript that at times seemed overwhelming is very much appreciated. Thank you also to Lara Kordic, who helped with the final polish and presentation.

I must also acknowledge the work of Ken Gibson and Leona Taylor in preserving the history of the west coast. Ken was willing to share photographs, documents, and his knowledge, and Leona's painstaking work in transcribing early news reports of the west coast into a searchable database saved days, probably weeks, of searching. My father, David Mason, a retired archivist, also offered me great support and set me on the right path more than once. Margaret Horsfield shared her own research on west coast history and was a much-valued sounding board and friend.

I am indebted to the following archivists and researchers: Kate Bird (*Vancouver Sun* and *Province*), Claudia Cole, Ulla Visscher, Pamela Manning (The Whyte Museum of the Canadian Rockies), Nancy Richards (Grand Valley State University), Cindy Van Volsem (Alberni Valley Museum), the team of archivists at the British Columbia Provincial Archives, and the volunteers of the Alberni Archives and the Ucluelet and Area Historical Society.

Thanks also to the following people who answered my questions, vetted draft sections, and otherwise assisted me: Arlene Armstrong, Roly Arnet, Ian Atherton, Barb Beasley, Danielle Bellefleur, Ann Branscombe, Lisa Brisco, Kim Brunt, Rob Butler, Barbara Campbell, Tom Curley, Adrian Dorst, Mark Fortune, Pamela Golby, Bob Hansen, Derek Hayes, Sibylla Helm, John Ingwersen Jr., Jody Klymak, John McIntosh, Alan McMillan, Andrew Mason, Margaret Mason, Ron Pododworny, Bob Redhead, Margaret Thompson, Jacqueline Windh, Jennifer Yakimishyn, and Chris Yorath.

The following people granted me interviews: Bruce Atkey, Norma Baillie, Pat Boland, Neil Buckle, John Burchett, Don Carmichael, Darlene Choquette, Allison Cronin, Jackie Cronin, Bill Dale, Jim Darling, Reg David, Jan Draeseke, Robin Fells, Kent Fiddy, Jennifer Fisher-Bradley, John Genn, Pamela Golby, George and Ruby Gudbranson, Roger and Anne Gudbranson, Walter Guppy, Mary Hardy, Les Hempsall, Frank and Lavern Hillier, Jim Hudnall, Vicky Husband, Brian Kimola, Steve Lovekin, Gordon and Sandra McClain, Jon Magwood, Jim Martin, Moses Martin, Bill and Val Mole, Warren Moraes, Doreen Myers, Frances Nakagawa, Doug Palfrey, Jeff Reves, Godfrey Stephens, Philip Thornton, Ralph Tieleman, Stan Tompkins, Barb Touchie, Len Walker, Barney Williams Sr., and Arlene Winpenny.

My thanks go as well to the BC Arts Council for their support.

Finally, thanks once again to my family—husband Bob, daughters Ava and Patrice—who have been more than patient and understanding over the years, particularly the last two, as I holed up in my office trying to tease another book to life. I know you share my enthusiasm and love for the place we are privileged to call our home, and I hope these stories will help bring even greater texture and understanding to the times we spend here.

selected references

RESEARCHING THIS BOOK was such a pleasure. A frustrating one at times, but there is something enticing to search and search and finally be rewarded with a new character or story or to confirm a fact you've been trying to verify for weeks. Often that "fact" added only a sentence, perhaps only a word or a date, to the final book. In the end it might have been cut, but still, the search was irresistible. The hardest thing to do was stop. My editors and publisher are, no doubt, glad that I finally did and got down to the business of writing.

I consulted dozens of books and hundreds of reports and newspaper articles to create *Long Beach Wild*. This list is only a partial one of the most relevant sources. For those who love the pursuit as I do, you can find a complete list at www.longbeach wild.com.

BOOKS

Abraham, Dorothy. *Lone Cone: Life on the West Coast of Vancouver Island, B.C.* Vancouver: privately printed, 1945.

Arima, E.Y. *The West Coast People: The Nootka of Vancouver Island and Cape Flattery.* Victoria, BC: British Columbia Provincial Museum, 1983.

Armia, E.Y., et al. *Between Ports Alberni and Renfrew: Notes on West Coast Peoples.* Canadian Ethnology Service, Mercury Series Paper 121. Hull, QC: Canadian Museum of Civilization, 1991.

Bossin, Bob. *Settling Clayoquot.* Sound Heritage Series #33. Victoria: Sound and Moving Image Division, BC Provincial Archives, 1981.

Brabant, Augustin. *Mission to Nootka: 1874–1900.* Charles Lillard (ed.). Sidney, BC: Gray's Publishing, 1977.

Brubacher, J., C. Cunningham, et al. *The Sound Anthology: News around Clayoquot Sound.* Tofino, BC: The Sound Magazine, 1997.

Cannings, Richard and Sydney Cannings. *British Columbia: A Natural History.* Vancouver: Greystone Books, 1996.

Carr, Emily. *Growing Pains: An Autobiography.* Toronto: Irwin, 1946.

Drucker, Philip. *The Northern and Central Nootkan Tribes.* Smithsonian Institution Bureau of American Ethnology Bulletin 144. Washington, DC: U.S. Government Printing Office, 1951.

Gibson, Gordon. *Bull of the Woods.* Vancouver: Douglas & McIntyre, 1980.

Gordon, Katherine. *Made to Measure: A History of Land Surveying in British Columbia.* Winlaw, BC: Sono Nis, 2006.

Guppy, Walter. *Wet Coast Ventures: Mine-Finding on Vancouver Island.* Victoria, BC: Cappis Press, 1988.

——. *Clayoquot Soundings: A History of Clayoquot Sound, 1880s-1980s.* Tofino, BC: Grassroots Publications, 1997.

——. *A Place for Gold.* Tofino, BC: Grassroots Publications, 2000.

——. *Eighty Years in Tofino.* Duncan, BC: Firgrove Publishing, 2002.

Hayes, Derek. *Historical Atlas of British Columbia and the Pacific Northwest.* Vancouver: Cavendish Books, 1999.

Hempsall, Leslie. *We Stand on Guard for Thee: A History of the War Years at the Royal Canadian Air Force Stations, Ucluelet and Tofino.* Surrey, BC: Coomber-Hempsall Publishing, 2003.

Hoover, Alan L. (ed.) *Nuu-chah-nulth Voices, Histories, Objects and Journeys.* Victoria, BC: Royal British Columbia Museum, 2000.

Horsfield, Margaret. *Voices From the Sound: Chronicles of Clayoquot Sound and Tofino 1889–1929.* Nanaimo, BC: Salal Books, 2008.

Lillard, Charles. *Seven Shillings a Year: The History of Vancouver Island.* Ganges, BC: Horsdal and Schubart, 1986.

McDiarmid, Howard. *Pacific Rim Park: A Country Doctor's Role in Preserving Long Beach and Establishing the New Wickaninnish Inn.* Victoria: Howard McDiarmid, 2009.

McNamee, James. *Florencia Bay.* London: New Authors Limited, 1960.

Moser, Charles. *Reminiscences of the West Coast of Vancouver Island.* Victoria: The Acme Press, 1926.

Murray, Peter. *The Vagabond Fleet: A Chronicle of the North Pacific Sealing Schooner Trade.* Victoria: Sono Nis, 1988.

Nicholson, George. *Vancouver Island's West Coast 1762–1962.* Victoria: Morriss Printing, 1962.

Peterson, Jan. *Journeys: Down the Alberni Canal to Barkley Sound.* Lantzville, BC: Oolichan Books, 1999.

Reid, Dennis. *Canadian Jungle: The Later Work of Arthur Lismer.* Toronto: Art Galley of Ontario, 1985.

Richards, George H. *Vancouver Island Pilot.* London: British Hydrographic Office, 1864.

Scott, Andrew. *The Encyclopedia of Raincoast Place Names.* Madeira Park, BC: Harbour Publishing, 2009.

Speedie, Julie. *Wonderful Sphinx: The Biography of Ada Leverson.* London: Virago Press, 1993.

Sproat, Gilbert Malcolm. *The Nootka: Scenes and Studies of Savage Life.* Edited and annotated by Charles Lillard. Victoria: Sono Nis Press, 1987.

Stewart, Hilary. *Cedar.* Vancouver: Douglas & McIntyre, 1984.

Stone, Jim. *My Dad, The Rum Runner.* Waterloo, ON: North Waterloo Academic Press, 2002.

Streetly, Joanna. *Salt in Our Blood: An Anthology of West Coast Moments.* Tofino, BC: Aquila Instincts, 2002.

Suttles, Wayne. (Ed.) *Handbook of North American Indians: Northwest Coast.* Washington, DC: Smithsonian Institute, 1990.

Walbran, John T. *British Columbia Coast Names 1592–1906: Their Origin and History.* Vancouver: Douglas & McIntyre, 1971.

Weicht, Chris. *Jericho Beach and the West Coast Flying Boat Stations.* Chemainus, BC: MCW Enterprises, 1997.

Wells, R.E. *A Guide to Shipwrecks: Cape Beale to Cox Point, Including Barkley Sound.* Sooke, BC: Morriss Printing, 1984.

Windh, Jacqueline. *The Wild Edge: Clayoquot, Long Beach & Barkley Sound.* Madeira Park, BC: Harbour Publishing, 2004.

Wyndham, Violet. *The Sphinx and Her Circle: A Biographical Sketch of Ada Leverson.* New York: Vanguard Press, 1963.

Yorath, Chris. *The Geology of Southern Vancouver Island.* Madeira Park, BC: Harbour Publishing, 2005.

ARTICLES/PAPERS/REPORTS

Numerous articles were consulted in the following papers: *Alberni Valley Times, Island Events, The Tofino-Ucluelet Press, Twin Cities Times* (Alberni and Port Alberni), *Vancouver Sun, Victoria Daily Colonist, Victoria Daily Times, West Coast Advocate* (Port Alberni), *Westcoaster* (Ucluelet-Tofino).

Ayre, Robert. "A Sheaf of Summer Sketches." *Canadian Art* 13, no. 2 (1956).

Banfield, W.E. "Banfield Explorations." An eight-part series originally published August 12 to September 17, 1858, in the *Victoria Daily Gazette.* Reprinted in the *Alberni Valley Times,* February 1984.

British Colonist. Accessed through database: Victoria's Victoria. www.victoriasvictoria.ca. 2007. (See Taylor and Mindenhall below.)

Clague, John J. "Tsunamis." In "A Synthesis of Geological Hazards in Canada," (ed.) G.R. Brooks. *Geological Survey of Canada, Bulletin 548* (2001): 27–42.

Clayoquot Sound Scientific Panel. "First Nations' Perspectives Relating to Forest Practices Standards in Clayoqout Sound." Appendices V and VI. 1995.

Guppy, Walter. "The Road to Tofino." *British Columbia Historical News* 33, no. 1 (1999): 16–18.

Hodgson, Ernest. "British Columbia Earthquake: June 23, 1946." *The Journal of the Royal Astronomical Society of Canada* XL, no. 8 (1946).

Hutchinson, Pat. "Census Taking at Wreck Bay, May–June 1971." *Cedar Bark and Sea.* Port Alberni: Ucluelet Recreation Commission. n.d.

McMillan, Alan and Ian Hutchinson. "When the Mountain Dwarfs Danced: Aboriginal Traditions of Paleoseismic Events Along the Cascadia Subduction Zone of Western North America." *Ethnohistory* 49, no. 1 (2002).

Mackie, Richard. "The Short, Happy Life and Sad Death of Fred Tibbs." *The Beaver,* February/March 1991.

Monashee Enterprises Ltd. v. Minister of Recreation and Conservation for the Province of British Columbia, [1978] Supreme Court of British Columbia, No. 467/1978 and No. 463/1978.

Smith, George A. "Reminscences of an Old Surveyor." *The Link* 11, no. 4 (1989).

PRIVATE DOCUMENTS:

Futcher, R.A. Memorandum re. Accidental Drownings at Long Beach, March 31, 1946. Courtesy Ken Gibson.

Hamilton, Mike. A Cruise in Clayoquot. Unpublished memoirs. n.d. Courtesy Ken Gibson.

——. Dream Isle and Its Owner. Unpublished memoirs. n.d. Courtesy Ken Gibson.

——. Oldtimer and Oldtimer's Son. Unpublished memoirs. n.d. Courtesy Ken Gibson.

Joint Road Committee. Letter to BC Minister of Public Works and other
documents related to the creation of Highway 4. Held in the Tofino
Public Library.

MacLeod, Ron. Growing Up in Tofino: Some Random Memories. 2002. Held in
the Tofino Public Library.

Scott, R. Bruce. How the Pacific Rim National Park Was Made. n.d. Held in the
Bruce Scott Collection, Pacific Rim National Park Reserve.

ARCHIVAL MATERIAL

BC ARCHIVES:

Buckle, Marilyn and Neil. 1979? Interview by Bob Bossin. Tape recording. Part
of Bob Bossin (Tofino-Clayoquot) oral history collection. T3878:0014-0015.

Carmichael, Alfred. Journal and Papers. MS 2305.

Dawley, Walter. Papers. MS 1076.

Donahue, Hazel. 1979? Interview by Bob Bossin. Tape recording. Part of Bob
Bossin (Tofino-Clayoquot) oral history collection. T3878:0026-0027.

Garrard, Francis C. Reminscences: 1863–1941. MS 0046.

Hillier, Bert and Peter. 1979? Interview by Bob Bossin. Tape recording. Part of
Bob Bossin (Tofino-Clayoquot) oral history collection. T3878:0040-0041.

Hillier, E.A. History of Ucluelet 1899 to 1954. MS 2169.

Jackson family fonds. Journals and guest book. MS 1113.

Martin, Phyllis. 1966. Interview by Imbert Orchard. Tape recording.
T0863:0001.

Moser, Charles. Diary, with edits by Dorothy Abraham. MS 2172.

Robertson, Alistair I. Report on Surveys in Clayoquot and Barclay Districts,
Vancouver Island. December 22, 1912. Microfiche reel XX, pp. D308-310.

Sloman, Alma. 1966. Interview by Imbert Orchard. Tape recording.
T0864:0001.

Whittington, Mary Margaret (Peg). 1979? Interview by Bob Bossin. Tape
recording. Part of Bob Bossin (Tofino-Clayoquot) oral history collection.
T3878:0033-0034.

OTHER ARCHIVES:

Banfield, William E. Oath of Allegiance and copies of reports to the Colonial
Secretary 1859–1862. Copies held at the Pacific Rim National Park Reserve
Archives, WRO #4033.

McCandless, R. Mrs. Mary (Peg) Whittington—Long Beach (Pacific Rim
National Park) in the Thirties and Forties: A Memoir. 1994. Pacific Rim
National Park Reserve Archives.

Murphy, Robert H. Commentary on George Jackson's Long Beach Diaries, January 1927 to May 1929. 1994. Pacific Rim National Park Reserve Historic
Manuscript Collection. HM-5.

Raue, A. and Barbara Hottson. Memories of hike to Long Beach in 1930.
Pacific Rim National Park Reserve Historic Manuscript Collection. HM-12.

Scott, R. Bruce. Pioneers of the Southwest Coast of Vancouver Island: A Series of
Translated Interviews. 1973. Bruce Scott Collection. Pacific Rim National
Park Reserve Archives. WRO 4082.

Taylor, Leona and Dorothy Mindenhall. Index of Historical Victoria
Newspapers, Victoria's Victoria. 2007. www.victoriasvictoria.ca.

Torrens, W. Copy of report submitted by W. Torrens to Colonial Secretary,
September 1865. Pacific Rim National Park Reserve Archives. WRO #4070.

Wardle, J.M. Report on Proposed National Park in Long Bay and Kennedy Lake
District, Vancouver Island, BC. Government of Canada: Canadian National
Parks Engineering Service. January 26, 1931. Pacific Rim National Park
Reserve Archive.

Whittington, Peg. Guest book of Singing Sands resort. Pacific Rim National
Park Reserve Historic Manuscript Collection. HM-XX.

Wickaninnish Provincial Park. Staff Summer Report. 1967. Pacific Rim
National Park Reserve Archive.

photo credits

205

82 courtesy Alberni Valley
   Museum Collection PN1036
84 courtesy Ucluelet and Area
   Historical Society
86 courtesy Ucluelet and Area
   Historical Society
90 Sander Jain
92 Adrian Dorst
96 (both) courtesy Parks Canada
99 (top) courtesy
   Anne Gudbranson
   (bottom) courtesy
   Parks Canada
100 courtesy Ucluelet and Area
   Historical Society
101 Gertrude Jackson photo,
   Ken Gibson Collection
104 courtesy Parks Canada
107 courtesy Parks Canada
109 Brian Kent/Vancouver Sun
110 courtesy Lovekin Family
113 courtesy Pamela Golby
118 Sander Jain
125 courtesy Parks Canada
131 courtesy Parks Canada
133 courtesy Parks Canada
134 courtesy Library and
   Archives Canada
137 Mark Hobson
139 George Redhead
140 Adrian Dorst
144 courtesy Pamela Golby
153 Alberni Valley Museum
   Collection PN10930
155 Bruce Mitchell
157 courtesy Ruth Sadler
159 The Province
164 Marnie Recker

169 courtesy Lovekin family
170 The Vancouver Sun
177 Brian Kent/Vancouver Sun
178 Brian Kent/Vancouver Sun
181 courtesy Parks Canada
182 Mary Christmas
183 (both) courtesy Parks Canada
188 Bob Hansen.

index

beachcombing, 7–8, 108–9
bears, 31, 89, *90*
Beautiful British Columbia, 94
Beddington, Ada, 88, 91
berries: in forest ecosystem, 55,
    119–20; in human diet, 30, 51, 97,
    98, 130, 160, 186; in wolf diet, 90
Billings, Bill, 180
Binns, Carl "Cap," 57, 58, *59*
birds, 37, 73, 75–76, *76*, 109
bogs, 119–21, 136
Bolingbroke Bomber, *134*
"The Bomber," 121, 135
bootleggers, 98, 106
bounties, for wolves and cougars, 89
Brabant, Augustin J., 49, 51
Bradley family (Merlin, Linda, Aaron),
    161, *182*
British Colonist (Victoria), 58, 60, 62
British explorers, traders, and settlers,
    42, 46, 48, 49, 51, 82–83.
    See also fur trade
Buckle, Neil, 19, 147, 149, 154, 174
Buckle family (Edgar, Evelyn, Neil,
    Dennis), 146–47
Burnt Lands, 77, 97, 123

California Current, 108
Campbell, Barry, 166
campgrounds, *81*, 155–56, 168, *183*
Camp Maquinna, *107*, 145, 147, 154
Canadian Dental Corps, 129
Canadian National Parks Association,
    167
canoes, 29–30, 32
Canso A 11007, "The Bomber,"
    121, 135
Cape Flattery, 50
Carelmapu, 66, 67, 70
Carmanah Creek, 68
Carmichael, Alfred, 63–65
Carr, Emily (Klee Wyck), *26*, 119

cars: amphibian casualties, 136;
    driving on the beach, 103–4, *104*,
    151–52, *153*, 163, *169*, *183*, 184, 186,
    187; of Hillier brothers, 101; of
    Jackson family, *99*; special cars,
    104. *See also* Highway 4; roads
Cascadia Subduction Zone, 15–16, 17
Choquette, Darlene, 162
Chrétien, Jean, 171, 172, *181*
Clamhouse, Louie, 17
clamming. *See* shellfish
Clayoquot First Nation. *See* Tla-o-
    qui-aht (Clayoquot) nation
Clayoquot Sound, *4*, 11, 14, 27, 41, 42,
    49
Clayoquot Sound Canning Company,
    78–79, 98
coastal forest. *See* temperate
    rainforest
coastal survey (1859), 47
Coast Construction Company, 123–
    24, 127–28
Cold War, military exercises, 149–50
Combers Beach, *4*, *141*
The Combers Resort, 147, 154,
    174, 176
communication links, 85–87
concretion, at Green Point, 8–9
Constance, HMS, 46
Cook, James, 25, 40–42
Cougar Annie, 89
cougars, 89–90, 193
Courtenay, earthquake (1946), 16
Cox Bay, 173
Cox Point, *4*, 5, 25
Crawford, Jeff, 154
culturally modified trees, 28–29,
    29, 30

Darling, Jim, 35, *35*, 162
Dawley, Walter, 80, 84, 97
Depression era, 102, 112, 115, 121–22

Trachuk, George, 180–81
Trans-Canada Highway, 102
transportation, to Long Beach, 143–
    45. *See also* roads
trees. *See* temperate rainforest
Triangle Island lighthouse, 83
Trudeau, Pierre, *109*, 176, *177*, *178*
Tseshaht people, 48
Ts'ishaa, 24
Tsonoqua myth, 119
tsunamis, 13–15, 16–19, 21
tukwnit (Sea Lion Rocks), 130, 190
"Tyee Jack" (Klih-wi-tu-a), 55, 57, 58

Uchuck, MV, 16, 143–44
Ucluelet, *4*, *26*; census and voters list,
    57, 62; Highway 4 impacts, 148;
    military bases, 122; missionaries
    and, 49, 51; road connections,
    86–87, 101, *104*; sawmill, 78;
    tsunami (1964), 19
Ucluelet First Nation. *See* Yuu-
    cluth-aht (Ucluelet) nation
Ucluelet Inlet, 48
Ucluelet Placer Mining Company, 58

Valdy, 162
Valencia, 66
Vancouver Island, geology of, 10–12,
    13–18
Vancouver Island Development
    League, 87
Vancouver Island Pilot, 47–48
Vargas Cone, 11
Vargas Island, *10*, 11
Victoria: earthquake (1946), 16;
    ferry service, 55; and gold rush,
    57, 58, 60, 62; as HBC fort, 46
Victoria Daily Colonist, 85, 87
Virgo, Sean, 162

Wardle, J.M., 167
water safety, 185. *See also* surfing;
    waves and surf
Water Safety and Surf Apparatus
    School, 185
waves and surf, 20, 93–95, *93*, 138–39,
    156–58. *See also* surfing; tsunamis
weather, 20, 62, 93–95, *93*, 105, 123.
    See also shipwrecks
Webb, Nellie and Joe, 145–46, 154
West Coast National Parks Act,
    172, 176
West Coast Trail, 68, 172
Western Air Command, 126
Western Forest Products, 54
western hemlocks, 68–69
western redcedar, 28–30, *29*, 68–69
whales, whaling, and whale-
    watching: First Nations traditions,
    30, 32–36, *37*, 192; grey whales, 24,
    34–35, *35*, 130, 190; humpback
    whales, 34; killer whales, 31;
    Pacific Rim Whale Festival, 34–35
Whittington, Peg and Dick: helped
    hippies, 162; Highway 4 impacts,
    152; hosted military personnel
    in WWII, 132–33; mine incident
    and Dick's death, 138–39, *139*, 163;
    reaction to national park, 168,
    173–74, 186–87; settled at Green
    Point, 112–15, *113*; Singing Sands
    resort, 115–16, 121, 143–44, *144*,
    154
Wickaninnish, Chief, 41, 42
Wickaninnish Bay, *4*, 11, 25
Wickaninnish Inn, 94, 154–55, *155*,
    172, 179–80
Wickaninnish Lodge, 145–46, 154
Wickaninnish Provincial Park,
    155–56, 168
Wilde, Oscar, 91

c